THE
PREEMINENT
CHRIST

THE
PREEMINENT
CHRIST

God's Beautiful and Unchanging Gospel

Paul Washer

Reformation Heritage Books
Grand Rapids, Michigan

The Preeminent Christ
© 2023 by Paul Washer

Reformation Heritage Books
3070 29th St. SE
Grand Rapids, MI 49512
616-977-0889
orders@heritagebooks.org
www.heritagebooks.org

Scripture taken from the New King James Version®. Copyright © 1982 by Thomas Nelson. Used by permission. All rights reserved.

Printed in the United States of America
23 24 25 26 27 28/10 9 8 7 6 5 4 3 2 1

Library of Congress Cataloging-in-Publication Data

Names: Washer, Paul, 1961- author.
Title: The preeminent Christ : God's beautiful and unchanging gospel / Paul Washer.
Description: Grand Rapids, Michigan : Reformation Heritage Books, [2023] | Includes bibliographical references.
Identifiers: LCCN 2022043671 (print) | LCCN 2022043672 (ebook) | ISBN 9781601789884 (hardcover) | ISBN 9781601789891 (epub)
Subjects: LCSH: Bible. Gospels. | Jesus Christ—Biography.
Classification: LCC BS2555.53 .W374 2023 (print) | LCC BS2555.53 (ebook) | DDC 226/.06—dc23/eng/20230103
LC record available at https://lccn.loc.gov/2022043671
LC ebook record available at https://lccn.loc.gov/2022043672

For additional Reformed literature, request a free book list from Reformation Heritage Books at the above regular or email address.

CONTENTS

FOREWORD

The gospel of Jesus Christ declares the unfathomable glory of God in the salvation of sinners, and the gospel itself is therefore inestimably glorious. That is not a trivial assertion.

Nothing in this vast universe of wonders is greater or more sublime than the glory of God. Moreover, God's glory is the ultimate *reason* for everything that exists. The universe and all that is in it was created for one principal objective—namely, to put the glory of God on display. Each one of us was made for that same purpose. Thus, the first question in the Westminster Shorter Catechism reminds us that our chief end is to glorify God and enjoy Him forever. Indeed, Scripture teaches us that the glory of God should dominate our awareness no matter what we might be doing at any given moment: "Whether you eat or drink, or whatever you do, do all to the glory of God" (1 Cor. 10:31).

Years ago a publisher asked me to contribute to a book in which several authors each explained and taught lessons from one favorite Bible verse. Since *all* Scripture is inspired and profitable for instruction in righteousness, there is not a single verse that I favor above all others. There are, however, several that I have a particular appreciation for because of their unusual clarity and sharp focus. Of these, the first verse that came to mind for my chapter in that book was 2 Corinthians 3:18: "We all, with unveiled face, beholding as in a mirror the glory of the Lord, are being transformed into the same image from glory to glory, just as by the Spirit of the Lord." That verse describes and illustrates how God's glory and the gospel message are inextricably bound together.

Divine glory is the theme that dominates what Paul is saying in the context surrounding 2 Corinthians 3:18. The apostle is making the point that the incarnate Christ is the living embodiment of God's glory. Moreover, he says, Christ shows us God's glory in a way that is infinitely superior to the occasional displays of shekinah glory we read about in the Old Testament. The physical display of glory in Moses's time was a glow so intense (and somewhat terrifying) that it had to be hidden behind a veil. In the gospel era, however, "the light of the knowledge of the glory of God [shines] in the face of Jesus Christ" (2 Cor. 4:6), and we can see it "with unveiled face" (3:18).

Hebrews 1:3 describes Christ as "the brightness of [God's] glory." Note, however, that the glory Christ reveals to us is much more than just the physical shining of a bright light. Christ Himself is "the image of the invisible God" (Col. 1:15), and He is the living perfection of "glory as of the only begotten of the Father, full of grace and truth" (John 1:14). He is "the true Light which gives light to every man" (1:9). His glory is evident not just through a visible shining but also in the purity of His holiness, the clarity and immutability of the truth He embodies, the moral beauty of His righteousness, and a host of other perfections.

Here is the most astonishing part: 2 Corinthians 3:18 says those who have Christ as their Lord and Savior are partakers of the divine glory. All believers are undergoing a process of transformation "from glory to glory" (from one degree of glory to the next). In short, we are being conformed to the likeness of Christ (Rom. 8:29). Unlike Moses, whose face temporarily bore a fading reflection of God's glory, we are being transformed by the Holy Spirit into Christlike vessels designed to put God's glory on display forever. The glory is not ours; it belongs to God alone, but because believers are indwelt by the Spirit of Christ, it is a glory that shines from within, not a mere reflection. Moses's glow at the foot of Sinai was a backscatter that soon grew dim and went away. In sharp contrast, the glory described in 2 Corinthians 3:18 grows stronger as time passes, and it will endure through eternity.

Thus, the gospel explains how it is possible for fallen, sinful people to be redeemed and remade into suitable vessels for God's own eternal glory. Gospel truth also opens the eyes of sinners so they can see and appreciate Christ's glory, and it transforms their minds and hearts to make them fit image bearers who by God's grace alone have a share in His eternal glory.

So it's fitting that the apostle refers to his message as "the gospel of the glory of Christ" (2 Cor. 4:4). Again, the gospel itself is *glorious*. In 1 Timothy 1:11, Paul refers to it as "the glorious gospel of the blessed God which was committed to my trust."

Because it conveys sinners safely to the glory of God (and is itself glorious), the gospel is a treasure worth more than all the riches of this world combined. So it is right that Paul saw the gospel as a precious doctrine to be closely guarded and faithfully, relentlessly disseminated to the world. He urged Timothy to guard it as well (1 Tim. 6:20). "Hold fast the pattern of sound words which you have heard from me.... That good thing which was committed to you, keep" (2 Tim. 1:13–14). Even beyond that, the apostle told his true son in the faith, "The things that you have heard from me among many witnesses, commit these to faithful men who will be able to teach others also" (2:2).

The glory and value of the gospel is too often underestimated and underappreciated, I fear, in the visible church today. I'm grateful for the voice and the pen of Paul Washer, who stands in stark contrast to the trifling superficiality of our generation. He understands and remains committed to the value and preeminence of the gospel, and he writes about it with passion and clarity.

I love what he has done in this book, skillfully explaining the gospel, describing its incredible legacy, demonstrating its inestimable worth, and arguing convincingly for the gospel to have its rightful place—*first* place—in the study, conversation, fellowship, and worship of Christians individually and the church collectively. I've written a number of books explaining, defending, and proclaiming the gospel. Paul Washer summarizes all of that neatly in this rich little volume that deserves to be read by every Christian who cares about the glory of God.

1

A PROLEGOMENON

The word *prolegomenon* is from the Greek verb *prolegein*, which means "to speak beforehand." In literature, it refers to a brief summary of a book's purpose and an explanation of the manner in which the author hopes to attain it.

It is a theological and philosophical maxim that a reasonable creature will chose the highest end or purpose for any endeavor. For the Christian writer, this great end or summum bonum (Latin: greatest good) must always be the glory or praise of God. As the apostle Paul commanded in 1 Corinthians 10:31, "Therefore, whether you eat or drink, or whatever you do, do all to the glory of God." Therefore, this brief work has been written for the glory and praise of God, and it will make much of Christ and His gospel.

The Glory of God

How can man do or write anything that would serve to bring glory to God? The psalmist asked, "What is man that You are mindful of him, and the son of man that You visit him?" (Ps. 8:4). When we compare God and man, it seems a great absurdity to think that the latter could bless the former or that the lesser could write anything that would bring glory to the greater (Heb. 7:7). Nevertheless, the Scriptures make it clear that we can and should glorify God in word and deed (1 Cor. 10:31). The Scriptures also instruct us that we are able to do so only to the degree that we speak or write according to what He has said about Himself (Isa. 8:20).

As unschooled as I am, this is my intention: to write about God as He has revealed Himself in the Scriptures, especially in the gospel of our Lord and Savior, Jesus Christ. Although God has made Himself known in many ways—creation, providence, law—the sum of these does not equal a tenth part of the gospel. It is in this singular message that God is most fully revealed and most fully known. For this reason, it is at the cross and the empty tomb that we will stake our claim and begin to mine. Each nugget of gold, diamond, and precious stone that is discovered is intended to enlarge our hearts so that we might esteem, believe, and praise God. As John Owen wrote, "The ultimate end of true theology is the celebration of the praise of God, and His glory and grace in the eternal salvation of sinners."[1]

Making Much of God

To glorify or praise God, we must know something of His manifest excellencies. These find their clearest expression in the person of Jesus Christ. In 2 Corinthians 4:6, the apostle Paul wrote that "the light of the knowledge of the glory of God" is found in the face of Christ. His meaning is unmistakable—the knowledge of God is most clearly revealed in the person of Jesus Christ and His great work of redemption on behalf of His people.

Without the slightest reservation or apology, the Scriptures declare Jesus of Nazareth and His death on Calvary to be the greatest revelation of God to men and angels. No matter how much light is seen in creation, the law, or God's works of providence, they are all a mere spark compared to the "Sun of Righteousness" and the light that He casts on the world (Mal. 4:2). Jesus declared, "He who has seen Me has seen the Father" (John 14:9), and the apostle Paul wrote, "For in Him dwells all the fullness of the Godhead bodily" (Col. 2:9). The writer of Hebrews also affirms that "[Christ is] the brightness of His glory and the express image of His person" (Heb. 1:3).

In accord with this great biblical, Reformed, and evangelical truth, we will seek to know God by knowing Christ and His gospel.

---

1. John Owen, *Biblical Theology* (Morgan, Pa.: Soli Deo Gloria, 1996), 619.

We will consider the preincarnate Son in glory, His incarnation, His perfect life, His suffering and death on Calvary, His resurrection, and finally His glorification and exaltation as the Savior, Lord, and Judge of all. Our sure hope is that the more we know of Christ, the more we will know of God, the greater will be our esteem for Him, and the more prevalent and pure will be our praise.

Although it is impossible to stretch a line across the expanse of Christ's infinitely glorious person, my desire has been to wear myself out in an earnest attempt to display Christ to you. If you finish with a greater knowledge of and esteem for Christ, then I will be content. As John Flavel wrote,

> If my pen were both able, and at leisure, to get glory in paper, it would be but a paper glory when I had gotten it; but if by displaying (which is the design of these papers) the transcendent excellency of Jesus Christ, I may win glory to Him from you, to whom I humbly offer them, or from any other into whose hands providence shall cast them, that will be glory indeed, and an occasion of glorifying God to all eternity.[2]

Please remember that we do not set forth Christ as an end in itself; it looks to a further purpose—that we might see Him and be forever captured by Him. The sinner's greatest need is to see Christ in the Scriptures through the regenerating and illuminating work of the Holy Spirit. As God declared through the prophet Isaiah, "Look unto me, and be ye saved, all the ends of the earth: for I am God, and there is none else" (Isa. 45:22 KJV). The Christian's greatest need is different but only by degrees. We need to see more of Christ so that we might be like Him (1 John 3:1). As the apostle Paul wrote, "But we all, with unveiled face, beholding as in a mirror the glory of the Lord, are being transformed into the same image from glory to glory, just as by the Spirit of the Lord" (2 Cor. 3:18).

---

2. John Flavel, *The Works of John Flavel* (Carlisle, Pa.: Banner of Truth, 1997), 1:xvii.

For the regenerate heart, there is a direct relationship between seeing more of Christ and being drawn closer to Him. The more God's people explore and discover the infinite excellencies of His person and work, the more they will love and be drawn to Him in communion and discipleship. Whether behind the pulpit or with pen in hand, this is the primary task of the expositor. It is for this reason that he withdraws from the multitude and enters his study to search the Scriptures for the precious stones of the gospel. Although he seeks to enrich his own heart, his greater passion is that God's people might see what he sees and be enthralled and constrained by it. As Hugh Martin wrote,

> And how does the true glory of a profound theology come out to view, as no dry, formal, abstract speculation; but the joyful handmaid, yea, the loving foster-mother, of spiritual life as in all the churches? It is when theology ransacks all her brightest treasures to turn them into arguments for charming and compelling men to come in, and frames her finest, richest theorems—refined and rich as aught that any scene has to show—into the powerful motives for the prisoner to come forth, and for them that sit in darkness to show themselves![3]

True exposition of the gospel is not less than an intellectual endeavor, but it is so much more. Its goal is that the mind might be engaged in great thoughts of God, that the heart might be inflamed with the love of God, that the body might be animated in service to God, and that the lips might be consecrated for the praise of God. This is the reason for this book. My desire is the same as that of Isaac Ambrose when he wrote in his introduction to his classic work, *Looking unto Jesus*,

> Oh! that all men, (especially into whose hands this book shall come) would presently fall upon the practice of this gospel art

3. Hugh Martin, *The Atonement: In Its Relations to the Covenant, the Priesthood, the Intercession of Our Lord* (Edinburgh: James Gemmell George IV. Bridge, 1882), 221.

of "looking unto Jesus!" If herein they find nothing of heaven, my skill will fail me; only let them pray, that as they look to Him, so virtue may go out of Him, and fill their souls.... A right beholding of Christ in His eternal workings will cause a desire of Christ above all desires; the heart now thirsts for nothing but Him that is all, all power, all love, all holiness, all happiness. Tell such a soul of the world, gold, and glory: Oh what are these? The soul will quickly tell you, the world is dung, and glory is dung, "all is but loss and dung for the excellency of the knowledge of Christ Jesus my Lord" [Phil. 3:8]. "Give me God and Christ," saith the soul, "or I die; oh my desires are to Him who hath done all this for me."[4]

---

4. Isaac Ambrose, *Looking unto Jesus: A View of the Everlasting Gospel* (Harrisonburg, Va.: Sprinkle Publications, 1986), viii, 75.

2

AN APOLOGY

The Oxford English Dictionary defines *apology* as "a regretful acknowledgment of a failure." Such an apology I must offer at the very outset of this book. No matter how knowledgeable or eloquent the preacher or how diligent and precise the writer, they are no match for the smallest part of the gospel of Jesus Christ. No one could count the grains of sand in the desert or the multitude of stars in the heavens, yet both tasks would be far easier than describing the excellencies and beauty of Christ and His gospel. John Newton wrote, "It is impossible that either men or angels can fully sound the depth of this one sentence, 'That Jesus Christ came into the world to save sinners' [1 Tim. 1:16]."[1] With this great truth William Bates concurred:

> Now the doctrine of the gospel excels the most noble sciences, as well contemplative as practical.... It affects the soul with the highest admiration. The strongest spirits cannot comprehend its just greatness: the understanding sinks under the weight of glory. The apostle who had seen the light of heaven, and had such knowledge as never any man before, yet, upon considering one part of the divine wisdom, breaks forth in astonishment, "Oh the depth of the riches of the wisdom and knowledge of God! how unsearchable are His decrees, and His ways past finding out!" [Rom. 11:33]. It is fit when we have spent the strength of our minds in the consideration

---

1. John Newton, *The Works of John Newton* (Carlisle, Pa.: Banner of Truth, 1988), 2:279.

of this excelling object, and are at the end of our subtlety, to supply the defects of our understandings with admiration; as the psalmist expresses himself, "Lord, how wonderful are thy thoughts to us-ward!"[2]

The writer and the preacher are prone to fail—yes, they are even destined to fail—because the subject of the discourse is beyond the minds and words of men and angels. Even when the preacher has spent his strength in study, poured out his soul in prayer, and exhausted himself in the pulpit, he must step down with bowed head knowing that the half, the tenth part, has not been told. This truth is well communicated by John Flavel:

> O fair sun, and fair moon, and fair stars, and fair flowers, and fair roses, and fair lilies, and fair creatures! But, oh ten thousand, thousand times fairer Lord Jesus! Alas, I wronged Him in making the comparison this way. Oh black sun and moon; but oh fair Lord Jesus! Oh black flowers, and black lilies and roses; but Oh fair, fair, ever fair Lord Jesus! Oh all fair things, black, deformed, and without beauty, when ye are set beside the fairest Lord Jesus! Oh black heaven, but oh fair Christ! Oh black angels, but oh surpassingly fair Lord Jesus![3]

The greatest hearts and minds of Christendom have not reached the foothills of the Everest that is the gospel. Even after an eternity of eternities in heaven we will not have reached the summit. This is not to say that the gospel cannot be understood savingly or even profoundly. It is simply an acknowledgment of its infinite nature. Even the apostle Paul admitted, "For now we see in a mirror, dimly" (1 Cor. 13:12) and "Oh, the depth of the riches both of the wisdom and knowledge of God! How unsearchable are His judgments and His ways past finding out!" (Rom. 11:33). Edward Payson wrote,

---

2. William Bates, *The Harmony of the Divine Attributes* (Birmingham, Ala.: Solid Ground Christian Books, 2010), 101–2.

3. Flavel, *Works of John Flavel*, 1:xix–xx.

That the gospel contains a grand display of the moral excellencies and perfections of Jehovah, will be denied by none, but the spiritually blind, who are ignorant of its nature. But to give only a general view of this grand display of God's character in a single discourse, or even in a volume, is impossible. With less difficulty might we enclose the sun in a lantern. We shall not, therefore, attempt to describe a subject, which must forever be degraded, not only by the descriptions, but by the conceptions, I will not say of men, but of the highest archangel before the throne. On no page less ample than that of the eternal, all-infolding mind, which devised the gospel plan of salvation, can its glories be displayed, nor by any inferior mind can they be fully comprehended.[4]

The seventeenth-century Puritan John Owen was one of the greatest theologians the church has ever known. His *Works*, which are contained in sixteen volumes, and his seven-volume commentary on Hebrews are without equal. However, recognizing the infinite greatness of the gospel that he sought so passionately to expound, he felt obligated to write the following in his book *Biblical Theology*:

It has been my professed intent and stated purpose—almost my one and only purpose in this work—to set forward the theology of Christ. This is not just the teaching of the gospel but the disposition of mind which alone can embrace it, and that goal has been ever present before my eyes from the start of this volume.... I personally do not claim to have attained to any great peak in the study of heavenly wisdom, or to be able to do more than stammer pitifully when I come to discuss or teach of such high matters. Here we are on ground where, at best, we can hope to see in part. Here is subject matter which the entire breadth of human intellect could never grasp; that is, until we cease to see through a glass darkly, and come to know even as we are known as we enjoy God without limit [1 Cor. 13:12]. There is little need of our denying our

---

4. Edward Payson, *The Complete Works of Edward Payson* (Harrisonburg, Va.: Sprinkle Publications, 1998), 3:42–43.

deep ignorance and shame of sloth when the same Apostle, in that epistle, admits that "If any man think that he knoweth anything, he knoweth nothing yet as he ought to know" [1 Cor. 8:2].[5]

If the likes of John Owen and even the great apostle Paul openly acknowledged their limited comprehension of the gospel and their near incapacity to expound it, how much more should I confess my ineptitude to address such a lofty matter. After I have spent all my strength and searched to the end of my abilities, I acknowledge that I have uncovered almost nothing in comparison to what remains to be seen. When I survey the gospel truths I have written in these pages, I am compelled to cry out with Job, "Indeed these are the mere edges of His ways, and how small a whisper we hear of Him" (Job 26:14)! When I review my presentation of these truths, I am compelled again to confess with Job that "I have uttered what I did not understand, things too wonderful for me, which I did not know" (42:3). However, I am consoled and encouraged by the words of John Flavel, who lamented the ineptitude of even the greatest scholars to display Christ in a manner worthy of Him:

> But let me tell you, the whole world is not a theatre large enough to shew the glory of Christ upon, or unfold the one half of the unsearchable riches that lie hid in Him. These things will be far better understood, and spoken of in heaven, by the noon-day divinity, in which the immediately illuminated assembly do there preach His praises, than by such a stammering tongue, and scribbling pen as mine, which doth but mar them. Alas! I write His praises but by moon-light; I cannot praise Him so much as by halves. Indeed, no tongue but His own (as Nazianzen said of Bazil) is sufficient to undertake that task. What shall I say of Christ? The excelling glory of that object dazzles all apprehension, swallows up all expression. When we have borrowed metaphors from every creature that hath any excellency or lovely property in it, till

---

5. Owen, *Biblical Theology*, 591.

we have stript the whole creation bare of all its ornaments, and clothed Christ with all that glory; when we have even worn out our tongues, in ascribing praises to Him, alas! we have done nothing, when all is done.[6]

In spite of certain failure, I must both write and speak, for "woe is me if I do not preach the gospel" (1 Cor. 9:16). Thus, being torn between my impotence to expound the gospel and my absolute necessity to do so, I commend this work to Christ's church collectively and to the believer individually. As Hugh Martin lamented when writing on the gospel, "I am ashamed to say these things, when I think how poor a contribution the following pages are to the discharge of the duty which I counsel. Still, I cast them, as my mite, into the treasury."[7] I will conclude this apology by offering good counsel to the reader from John Bunyan's conclusion to his classical work *The Pilgrim's Progress*:

> What of my dross thou findest here, be bold,
>   To throw away, but yet preserve the gold.
> What if my gold be wrapped up in ore?
>   None throws away the apple for the core.
> But if thou shalt cast all away as vain,
> I know not but 'twill make me dream again.[8]

---

6. Flavel, *Works of John Flavel*, 1:xviii.

7. Hugh Martin, *The Shadow of Calvary* (Carlisle, Pa.: Banner of Truth Trust, 2016), 9–10.

8. John Bunyan, *The Pilgrim's Progress* (Carlisle, Pa.: Banner of Truth Trust, 2017), 190.

3

THE ESSENTIAL CONTENT
OF THE GOSPEL

The word *gospel* is one of the most frequently used terms in the Christian vocabulary. However, the true power of this word is manifested only to the degree that we understand its biblical meaning. There is one sense in which the gospel is found on every page of the Scriptures. There is another in which it refers to a very distinct and unique message that is centered on the person and redemptive work of Jesus Christ, the Son of God. It is in this latter sense that I intend to employ the word *gospel* in this study.

As we go through the pages of Scripture, we will learn that the gospel is not a message among many but rather *the* message above them all. It is to be studied, cherished, and proclaimed as the greatest revelation of God to man, the only message of salvation given to man, and the great means by which the Christian is transformed and conformed to the nature and will of God.

Defining Terms

The word *gospel* is derived from the Old English word *godspel* (*gōd* [good] + *spel* [news, story]). Contrary to popular opinion, the Old English word *gōd* has a long ō and is a reference not to God but to that which is good. It does not mean "God's news" but "good news." In the New Testament, *gospel* is translated from the Greek word *euangélion* (*eù* [good] + *aggéllō* [to proclaim]). It denotes good new, joyful news, or glad tidings. In ecclesiastical Latin, *gospel* is translated *bona annuntiatio* (good announcement) or *bonus nuntius* (good message).

In this chapter, we will briefly consider the essential elements of the gospel so that we might begin our study with a working definition. However, before advancing any further, the reader must firmly grasp one great truth: the gospel is good news and should be proclaimed as such. Although a biblical presentation of the gospel will address many grave themes—sin, divine wrath, condemnation, and death—these themes are not an end in themselves but are a means to showcase the grace of God and the salvation He offers.

Two passages in the New Testament most encapsulate the goodness and joy that are inherent in the gospel message. The first text is found in Luke 2:9–10: "And behold, an angel of the Lord stood before them, and the glory of the Lord shone around them, and they were greatly afraid. Then the angel said to them, 'Do not be afraid, for behold, I bring you good tidings of great joy which will be to all people.'"

Whenever a holy God draws near to sinful man, even in the form of a messenger, there is a reason for fear. Has God come with an olive branch of peace or with a sword of judgment? When the prophet Samuel drew near to Bethlehem, "the elders of the town trembled at his coming, and said, 'Do you come peaceably?'" (1 Sam. 16:4–5). If the leaders of a city showed such fear before an old man like themselves, we can only imagine the fear that struck the hearts of the shepherds when they found themselves in the very presence of the angel of the Lord. What a relief it must have been for them to hear that the angel came from God with "good tidings of great joy." Those of us who are called to the gospel ministry must always remember that we have been sent out with these same good tidings. Although we must deal with weighty matters, even those that are grievous and painful, we are to offer the promise of salvation to all who will repent and believe. Our message is only condemning to those who reject it.

The second text that powerfully communicates the goodness and joy of the gospel is found in Romans 10:15, where the apostle Paul quoted from Isaiah 52:7: "How beautiful [or lovely] are the feet of those who preach the gospel of peace."

First, notice the repetition. It would be extremely difficult for Isaiah or Paul to give greater emphasis to the goodness of the gospel and remain within the bounds of proper grammar. They are pushing language to its limits in order to communicate that the gospel is the very best of news. Second, take note of the word *beautiful* or *lovely*. The gospel is such good news to the discerning and believing heart that it is said to "beautify" or "make lovely" even the calloused and soiled feet of the messenger who brings it!

Imagine the fear and hopelessness of a condemned prisoner only moments before his execution. But as the hangman tightens the noose, a messenger runs up the stairs of the gallows, crying out, "Good news! Good news! The king has granted pardon!" Although the messenger is soaked in sweat and the mire of the street, he is beautified by his message and the prisoner embraces him without reservation.

Or imagine a small city-state that finds an immense army gathered at it borders intent on murder and pillage. In response, the king musters his army to meet the oncoming horde. Each day that passes without news seems to secure the city's doom. Then a single runner approaches from afar. The citizens gasp in horror. "Has the king and his entire army perished? Has only one man survived to carry back to the city a message of death?" When the last flicker of hope is utterly extinguished, they suddenly hear the voice of the messenger: "Good news! Good news! The king has triumphed! The enemy has been routed! You will live and not die!" The messenger is soiled with the blood and stench of battle, but he is beautified by the message he carries and is received with open arms and shouts of joy.

God could not have chosen a more excellent word than *gospel* to describe the redemptive work of His Son. Having conquered death, hell, and the grave, He now sends His envoys to the farthest corners of the world to announce the good news of His victory and the salvation He has won for His people!

Essential Elements
Throughout both the Old and New Testaments, the Scriptures contain various summary statements regarding the content of the gospel.

A few of the most important are found in Genesis 3:15; Isaiah 53:1–12; John 3:16–17; Romans 3:25–26; 1 Corinthians 15:3–4; and 2 Corinthians 5:21. In this book we will consider each of these texts in depth, along with many others. However, for now, and for the sake of introduction, I will briefly point out the major or essential elements of the gospel as they are set forth in the Scriptures.

The Character of God

One cannot understand reality apart from understanding who God is. Thus, in Proverbs 9:10 we read, "The knowledge of the Holy One is understanding." This is especially true with regard to the gospel of Jesus Christ. We simply cannot understand the gospel correctly apart from understanding something of the character of God. Why must Christ die? Because God is holy and righteous. Why did Christ die? Because God is love! Both questions find their answer in the character of God.

It is often stated that man's greatest problem is sin. This statement is not wrong, but it is incomplete. Sin would not be a hindrance to fellowship with God if He were amoral or immoral. Sin is a problem because God is holy and righteous. In fact, the entire gospel has to do with reconciling God's righteousness, which demands the punishment of the guilty (Ex. 34:7), with His mercy, which takes no pleasure in the death of the wicked (Ezek. 18:23; 33:11). How can God exercise mercy yet punish the wicked? How can He be both loving and just? The answer is found only in the person and work of Christ, who bore the sin of His people, suffered the wrath of God in their stead, and satisfied the demands of God's justice that was against them. This is the heart of the gospel, yet it can be understood only in the light of the revelation of the character of God!

The Depravity of Man

To properly understand the gospel, we must also understand and submit to the Scriptures' testimony regarding the moral depravity of man and his relentless rebellion against God. Adam was made in the *imago Dei*, or image of God (Gen. 1:27). However, his rebellion against God and subsequent fall from his original state of righteousness resulted in the fall of humanity and the corruption of the physical universe (Rom. 5:12; 8:20–22). Although something of God's image remains (James 3:9), humanity bears Adam's guilt, possesses his morally depraved nature, and willingly participates in his rebellion (Gen. 5:3; 8:21; Rom. 3:10–23; Eph. 2:1–3; 4:17–19). As a result, humanity is separated from fellowship with God and is under His righteous wrath (John 3:36; Rom. 1:18). From our side, reconciliation with God is an absolute impossibility, but "the things which are impossible with men are possible with God" (Luke 18:27). He has provided salvation through the death and resurrection of His. Son. The gospel of Jesus Christ does not ignore or downplay our sin but rather brings it to the forefront in all its ugliness and deals with it in the cross (Isa. 53:4–6, 10; 1 Peter 2:24; 3:18). If we eliminate or make light of this essential truth of the gospel, we will have perverted its content, truncated its power, and brought judgment on ourselves (Gal. 1:8–9)!

Christ's Person and Preincarnate Glory
The gospel is the historic account of God the Son becoming flesh (John 1:1), dwelling among sinful men (John 1:14), and suffering and dying as a vicarious or substitutionary sacrifice for His people (Matt. 27:50; Mark 15:37; Luke 23:46; John 19:30). This wonderful act has often been called a humiliation or an emptying. However, none of these terms can fully communicate the greatness of the Son's condescension unless we first understand something of the greatness of His preincarnate glory. It was not a mere man, an archangel, or even a demigod that suffered and died on Calvary. It was the very One whom Isaiah saw "sitting on a throne, high and lifted up, and the train of His robe filled the [heavenly] temple," the One who was surrounded by the seraphim, who covered their faces and cried out to Him, "Holy, holy, holy is the LORD of hosts; the whole earth is full of His glory!" (Isa. 6:1–3; see also John 12:41).

It is a great deed for one man to give his life for another. But for the Son of God, the Creator and Sustainer of the universe, to give His life for sinful man is incomprehensible. In Romans 5:7–8 the apostle Paul argued, "For scarcely for a righteous man will one die; yet perhaps for a good man someone would even dare to die. But God demonstrates His own love toward us, in that while we were still sinners, Christ died for us." The more we understand something of the infinite, eternal glory of the Son, the more we will comprehend the greatness of His humiliation and the greater will be our esteem for Him. Only then will we be able to sing with understanding the words of Charles Wesley, "Amazing love! How can it be, that Thou my God, shouldst die for me?"[1]

Christ's Incarnation

The word *incarnation* refers to the Son of God being conceived in the womb of the virgin Mary by the power of the Holy Spirit (Luke 1:35) and being born the God-man, Jesus of Nazareth. In this incarnation, the eternal Son became a true man in every sense of the term yet remained fully God. As the apostle Paul wrote, "For in Him dwells all the fullness of the Godhead bodily" (Col. 2:9). The incarnation is an absolutely essential doctrine of the gospel and one of its greatest storehouses of glory. On one hand, Christ had to be man. Man has sinned and man must die. The sacrifice must be made in the same nature as that in which the crimes were committed, "for it is not possible that the blood of bulls and goats could take away sins" (Heb. 10:4). On the other hand, Christ had to be God. A mere man, an angel, or even some sort of demigod would not have been sufficient. A sacrifice of infinite worth and perfect inherent righteousness was required—a worth and a righteousness possessed by God alone. Thus, Paul testified that in Christ, God purchased the church "with His own blood" (Acts 20:28), and "God was in Christ reconciling the world to Himself" (2 Cor. 5:19). The glories contained in the incarnation will take an eternity of eternities to sound out, but a more noble labor cannot be found. The more we comprehend what it means for God to become man and for that man to be Immanuel

---

1. Charles Wesley, "And Can It Be That I Should Gain," 1738.

(God with us), the greater will be our devotion, the more complete and enduring our obedience, and the more vibrant our proclamation and worship.

Christ's Perfect Obedience

Many theologians have regarded Christ's perfect obedience as His greatest miracle, yet it is often overlooked as an essential doctrine of the gospel. Christ's perfect obedience was necessary not only so that He might die for the sins of the unrighteous but also that His perfect life might be imputed to the disobedient. In Psalm 15:1, the psalmist asked, "LORD, who may abide in Your tabernacle? Who may dwell in Your holy hill?" In verse 2, the answer is given: "He who walks uprightly, and works righteousness, and speaks the truth in his heart." Again, in Psalm 24:3 the same question is set forth: "Who may ascend into the hill of the LORD? Or who may stand in His holy place?" In verse 4, the answer again is the same: "He who has clean hands and a pure heart, who has not lifted up his soul to an idol, nor sworn deceitfully." For God's people to stand fully accepted in His presence requires more than forgiveness or a clean slate. We must possess a perfect righteousness—a record of perfect conformity to the nature and will of God. But how is this to be obtained? The Scriptures testify that "there is none righteous, no, not one" (Rom. 3:10) and that "all our righteousnesses are like filthy rags" (Isa. 64:6). The good news is not only that Christ offered His perfect life as a sacrifice to atone for our sins but that His perfect life was imputed to us or reckoned to be ours the moment we believed. We who were destitute or naked of personal righteousness have now been clothed in the perfect righteousness of Christ. As the apostle Paul wrote, "He made Him who knew no sin to be sin for us, that we might become the righteousness of God in Him" (2 Cor. 5:21), and again, "[Christ] became for us wisdom from God—and righteousness and sanctification and redemption" (1 Cor. 1:30). He is "THE LORD OUR RIGHTEOUSNESS" (Jer. 23:6).

Christ's Death

The death of Christ is *the* great essential of all gospel essentials. However, it is not enough to believe and preach that Christ died; we must also understand and accept the purpose and meaning of His death as it is revealed to us in the Scriptures. It is an undeniable historical fact that Jesus of Nazareth died under Pontius Pilate outside the city of Jerusalem. Nevertheless, we have arrived at a biblical faith only when we recognize the vicarious nature and redemptive purpose of His death. Jesus did not die as a martyr. Nor did He die merely as an affirmation of divine love or as an example to be followed by His disciples. Christ died *for* His people, *on behalf of* His people, *in place of* His people, and as a *substitute* for His people. On Calvary, He bore our sins, suffered the wrath of God against us, and died under the penalty of the law. In this way, He satisfied the demands of God's righteousness that were against us, appeased God's wrath, and made it possible for God to pardon our sin without the least violation of His righteousness. On the cross, Christ experienced untold physical suffering. However, it was not merely the lacerations on His back, the crown of thorns on His head, or the nails in His hands and feet that purchased our salvation. We are not saved merely because of what men did to Jesus; we are saved because of what God the Father did to His only Son. He reckoned or imputed to Jesus our sin and treated Him as guilty (Isa. 53:6; 2 Cor. 5:21). The Father withdrew His favorable presence from Christ (Matt. 27:46) and crushed Him under the divine wrath that was due us. As it was described by the prophet Isaiah, "It pleased the LORD to bruise Him; He has put Him to grief. When You make His soul an offering for sin" (Isa. 53:12). To believe any other so-called theory of man or angel regarding the death of Christ is to deny the gospel and to subject oneself to eternal condemnation. In Galatians 1:8–9, Paul was very emphatic: "But even if we, or an angel from heaven, preach any other gospel to you than what we have preached to you, let him be accursed. As we have said before, so now I say again, if anyone preaches any other gospel to you than what you have received, let him be accursed." For this reason, the great bulk of the material in this book is devoted to setting forth and explaining the death of Christ. Our goal is twofold: first, that we stand fast in "the faith which was once for all delivered to the saints" (Jude 3), and second, that even the faintest whisper of Calvary might draw out our greatest affections and compel us to the most earnest and sincere devotion to Christ.

Christ's Resurrection

It is not enough to believe and preach biblically about the death of Christ. We must also believe and preach that on the third day He was raised from the dead in the same physical body in which He died (John 20:27). This truth is absolutely essential to the gospel and the Christian faith. It is nonnegotiable! If Christ did not physically rise from the dead, then the whole of Christianity is a lie. The apostle Paul wrote, "If Christ is not risen, then our preaching is empty and your faith is also empty.... And if Christ is not risen, your faith is futile; you are still in your sins" (1 Cor. 15:14, 17). It is for this reason that the central theme of the book of Acts is the proclamation of Christ's resurrection. The people of the apostolic era knew very well that a man named Jesus of Nazareth had died on a cross outside the gates of Jerusalem, but the proof that His death was God's greatest work of redemption resided in the historical accuracy of His resurrection, which the early Christians believed and proclaimed, even in the face of ridicule and threat.

According to the Scriptures, Christ's resurrection is God's public declaration of Jesus's sonship (Rom. 1:4), the confirmation of our justification (Rom. 4:25), the validation of our faith (1 Cor. 15:13–14), the pledge of our future resurrection (John 14:19), and the proof that God will bring all men to judgment (Acts 17:31).

In light of Scripture's emphasis on the absolute essentiality of Christ's bodily resurrection, it is astounding how often it has been denied or "modified" even by those who have identified themselves with Christianity. Nevertheless, if we are to remain true to the apostolic gospel, we must proclaim Christ's vicarious death on Calvary and His bodily resurrection from the dead. Anything less than this is not a mere variation of the gospel but an outright denial of it!

Christ's Exaltation

The Scriptures teach not only that Christ died, was buried, and was raised but also that forty days after His resurrection He ascended into heaven and sat down at the right hand of God. The writer of Hebrews stated, "When He had by Himself purged our sins, sat down at the right hand of the Majesty on high" (1:3). The apostle Paul wrote, "He [i.e., God] raised Him from the dead and seated Him at His right hand in the heavenly places, far above all principality and power and might and dominion, and every name that is named, not only in this age but also in that which is to come" (Eph. 1:20–21) and "God also has highly exalted Him and given Him the name which is above every name, that at the name of Jesus every knee should bow, of those in heaven, and of those on earth, and of those under the earth, and that every tongue should confess that Jesus Christ is Lord, to the glory of God the Father" (Phil. 2:9–11).

The Old Testament prophecies concerning the Messiah also concur with these apostolic affirmations. God declared through the psalmist, "I have set My King on My holy hill of Zion" (Ps. 2:6) and again through Isaiah, "I will divide Him a portion with the great, and He shall divide the spoil with the strong" (Isa. 53:12). The prophet Daniel is even more explicit: "To Him was given dominion and glory and a kingdom, that all peoples, nations, and languages should serve Him. His dominion is an everlasting dominion, which shall not pass away, and His kingdom the one which shall not be destroyed" (Dan. 7:14).

The Son of God, who was made in the likeness of men and became obedient even to the point of death on a cross (Phil. 2:7–8), has now been exalted as the sovereign Lord and Judge of all and the Savior and Mediator of His people. In the preaching of the apostles, this great truth held a prominent place beside the death and resurrection of Christ and should hold an equally prominent place in ours. God has installed His King on Zion. He has given Him the nations as His inheritance and the very ends of the earth as His possession. Furthermore, He has granted Him absolute sovereignty over all (Ps. 2:6–9). For this reason, the gospel message contains not only the free offer of salvation to all but a solemn warning even to the greatest kings and nations of the earth: "Now therefore, be wise, O kings; be instructed, you judges of the earth. Serve the LORD with fear, and rejoice with trembling. Kiss the Son, lest He be angry, and you perish in the way, when His wrath is kindled but a little. Blessed are all those who put their trust in Him" (Ps. 2:10–12).

Christ's Return

According to the Scriptures, human history is linear, with a fixed and purposeful beginning and ending. From the first day of creation, God has been directing every person and event to a specific culmination or climax—the second coming of our Lord and Savior Jesus Christ, the judgment of the world, and the establishment of a new heaven and earth. The purpose for giving prominence to this great truth in our gospel proclamation is twofold. First, it is to encourage the believer to go on believing and to live with the hope of a future grace and glory that far surpasses our present powers of comprehension: "Eye has not seen, nor ear heard, nor have entered into the heart of man" (1 Cor. 2:9). Second, it is to warn the unbeliever. We must always remember that a proper proclamation of the gospel will include a call to all men to "prepare to meet your God" (Amos 4:12). The apostle Paul declared to the philosophers on Mars Hill, "[God] has appointed a day on which He will judge the world in righteousness by the Man whom He has ordained. He has given assurance of this to all by raising Him from the dead" (Acts 17:31).

The second coming is a doctrine that is replete with contrasting extremes. For some, it will be a day of salvation—"joy inexpressible and full of glory" (1 Peter 1:8). For others it will be a day of doom in which they will hide themselves in the caves and among the rocks of the mountains, and they will cry out to the mountains and the rocks, "Fall on us and hide us from the face of Him who sits on the throne and from the wrath of the Lamb! For the great day of His wrath has come, and who is able to stand?" (Rev. 6:16–17). For this reason, the gospel messenger is also something of a contrast. To those who believe, he is "an aroma of life leading to life," but to those who refuse to believe he is "an aroma of death leading to death." It was this solemn reality that caused the apostle Paul to cry out, "Who is sufficient for these things?" (2 Cor. 2:16).

Knowing that so much hangs in the balance, and that the gospel alone has the power to save (Rom. 1:16), should we not "meditate on these things; give [ourselves] entirely to them, that [our] progress may be evident to all" (1 Tim. 4:15)? Should we not "be diligent to present [ourselves] approved to God, a worker who does not need to be ashamed, rightly dividing the word of truth" (2 Tim. 2:15)?

A Call to Repentance and Faith

The gospel message is not complete without a call for all people everywhere to respond by repenting of their sin and believing or trusting exclusively in the person and work of Jesus Christ. In the gospel of Mark we are given the very first account of Jesus's ministry. Mark wrote, "Jesus came to Galilee, preaching the gospel of the kingdom of God, and saying, 'The time is fulfilled, and the kingdom of God is at hand. Repent, and believe in the gospel'" (Mark 1:14–15). To the philosophers in Athens, the apostle Paul declared, "Truly, these times of ignorance God overlooked, but now commands all men everywhere to repent" (Acts 17:30). To the church in Ephesus, Paul affirmed, "I kept back nothing that was helpful, but proclaimed it to you, and taught you publicly and from house to house, testifying to Jews, and also to Greeks, repentance toward God and faith toward our Lord Jesus Christ" (Acts 20:20–21). This twofold call of the gospel is also affirmed by the greatest confessions of church history. The Westminster Confession states, "Repentance unto life is an evangelical grace; the doctrine thereof is to be preached by every minister of the Gospel, as well as that of faith in Christ."[2] The New Hampshire Confession of Faith likewise says, "We believe that repentance and faith are sacred duties, and also inseparable duties."[3]

---

2. The Westminster Confession of Faith (Glasgow, Scotland: Free Presbyterian Publications, 1995), 15.1.

3. John Brown, The New Hampshire Confession of Faith (1833), VIII, in

The preaching of the gospel is more than a mere communication of information. It is an earnest and urgent call for men to be saved from eternal destruction through repentance and faith in Christ. This truth is best illustrated in the preaching of the apostle Paul, who penned the following words to the church in Corinth: "We are ambassadors for Christ, as though God were pleading through us: we implore you on Christ's behalf, be reconciled to God" (2 Cor. 5:20).

William L. Lumpkin, *Baptist Confessions of Faith* (Valley Forge, Pa.: Judson Press, 1969), 364.

4

THE SAME GOSPEL
THROUGH THE AGES

Throughout church history, sincere Christians, preachers, and scholars have sought to identify and summarize the essentials of the Christian faith in concise and intelligible statements. In many of these creeds and confessions, the gospel is presented with amazing clarity, giving us something of a standard for historical Christian interpretation. These creeds and confessions are not inspired, inerrant, or infallible; they must not be set above or equal to the Scriptures in authority. Nevertheless, they were written for the purpose of instruction and to protect the church from heresy. Therefore, they are useful for every generation of Christians because they are a record of what orthodox believers have affirmed throughout the centuries. The purpose for citing the following creeds and confessions is not to endorse those who wrote them or to affirm every detail of their content. It is simply to demonstrate two important realities: first, that the gospel holds the central place in the doctrines of historical Christianity, and second, that the essential tenets of the gospel have been affirmed by genuine believers throughout the long history of the church.

An important principle of hermeneutics is that we should study the Scriptures in the context of the church. From the apostolic era until the present, there have been believers who have revered, loved, and studied the Scriptures. They represent nearly two millennia of interpretation that serves not only as instruction but also as a subordinate standard by which we might compare our own private or personal interpretations. If all the Bible-believing Christians throughout history are in agreement with regard to a certain interpretation of the Bible but our personal interpretation or that of our generation differs from them, it should be a red flag to warn us that we may be in error and should reconsider our opinions.

As we study the Scriptures, we must always remember three important truths. First, the Bible is the only inspired, inerrant, and infallible word of God, and nothing should be set above or beside it. All creeds and confession should be considered as subordinate in authority to the Scriptures themselves. It is for this reason that they are often referred to as "subordinate" or "secondary" standards. Second, wisdom was not born with us and it will not die with us. Although our Bibles are inspired, our personal interpretations are not. It is a great display of arrogance to isolate ourselves from two thousand years of church history and interpret the Bible in a personal vacuum. Third, anyone who has studied the great writings of church history (especially those of the Reformers, Puritans, and early evangelicals) will not only recognize their great worth but also be humbled by the depth, breadth, and height of their knowledge and piety as compared to our present generation.

Throughout this book, the reader will be aided (and, we hope, blessed) by excerpts of commentaries and treatises written by men and assemblies from the long history of the church. However, we must never forget that our primary concern is with the simple exposition of the Scriptures themselves. They alone are the highest authority and standard regarding all matters of faith, doctrine, and practice. With this truth, the greatest confessions and creeds ever written are in complete agreement. The first chapter of the esteemed 1689 London Baptist Confession begins and ends with these words:

> The Holy Scripture is the only sufficient, certain, and infallible rule of all saving knowledge, faith, and obedience.... The supreme judge, by which all controversies of religion are to be determined, and all decrees of councils, opinions of ancient writers, doctrines of men, and private spirits, are to be examined, and in whose sentence we are to rest, can be no other

but the Holy Scripture delivered by the Spirit, into which Scripture so delivered, our faith is finally resolved.[1]

The Apostles' Creed

The Apostles' Creed is the oldest of the preserved Christian creeds. Its original form and content most likely dates from the early part of the second century (approximately AD 120). Although there is no historical evidence for the assumption that it was written or redacted by the twelve apostles, it does provide the core beliefs of the apostolic faith, especially with regard to the gospel. It was most likely used for the instruction of new converts and as a safeguard against the prevailing heresies of the day (Marcionism, Gnosticism, Docetism). Regarding the influence of the Apostles' Creed, theologian Joel Beeke writes, "The Reformers frequently incorporated the Apostles' Creed into their worship and liturgy. More than any other Christian creed, it may justly be called an ecumenical symbol of faith, for until the present day it is the most widely used confessional statement in the Western or Latin Church."[2]

The following portion of the Apostles' Creed sets forth the content of the gospel. It affirms faith in the triune God; Christ's deity and incarnation; Christ's death, resurrection, and ascension; and Christ's universal judgment. The creed states,

> I believe in God the Father, Almighty,
> Maker of heaven and earth;
> And in Jesus Christ, His only begotten Son, our Lord;
> Who was conceived by the Holy Spirit,
> Born of the Virgin Mary;
> Suffered under Pontius Pilate;
> Was crucified, dead and buried;
> He descended into hell;

---

1. The 1689 London Baptist Confession of Faith, 1.1, 10, in *The Baptist Confession of Faith and the Baptist Catechism* (Vestavia Hills, Ala.: Solid Ground Christian Books; and Carlisle, Pa.: Reformed Baptist Publications, 2010), 1, 5.

2. Joel Beeke, *The Three Forms of Unity* (Vestavia Hills, Ala.: Solid Ground Christian Books, 2012), 4.

The third day He rose again from the dead;
He ascended into heaven,
And sitteth at the right hand of God the Father
    Almighty;
From thence He shall come to judge the quick
    and the dead....

As stated above, my purpose for citing these creeds and confessions is simply to demonstrate that the principal tenets of the gospel have been affirmed by genuine believers throughout the long history of Christianity.

The Nicene Creed

The Nicene Creed was written to protect the orthodox faith against the great heresies of the fourth and fifth centuries, especially Arianism, which denied the Trinity and the deity of Christ. The roots of the creed reach back to the Council of Nicaea in AD 325, which was convened to affirm the answer to the most profound question facing the Christian church: "Who is Jesus Christ?" The creed went through significant revision at the Council of Constantinople in AD 381 and was accepted as a definitive statement of the Christian faith at the Council of Chalcedon in AD 451.

The following portion of the Nicene Creed presents the content of the gospel. Although it is more detailed than the Apostles' Creed, it affirms the same tenets listed above:

I believe in one God, the Father Almighty,
Maker of heaven and earth, and of all things visible
    and invisible.

And in one Lord Jesus Christ, the only-begotten Son of God,
begotten of the Father before all worlds;
God of God, Light of light, very God of very God;
begotten, not made, being of one substance with the Father,
    by whom all things were made.
Who, for us men for our salvation,
    came down from heaven,

and was incarnate by the Holy Spirit of the virgin Mary,
and was made man;
and was crucified also for us under Pontius Pilate;
He suffered and was buried;
and the third day He rose again, according to the Scriptures;
and ascended into heaven, and sitteth on the right hand of
the Father;
and He shall come again with glory, to judge the quick and
the dead;
whose kingdom shall have no end.

The Belgic Confession

The Belgic Confession of Faith is one of the oldest confessions of the Reformed faith and is renowned for its clarity, profundity, and beauty. It was written in the sixteenth century by Guido de Brès (1522–1567) and fellow pastors of the Reformed persuasion in the Netherlands who were undergoing severe persecution at the hands of Philip II of Spain and the Roman Catholic Church.

The Belgic Confession was received as the doctrinal standard of the Reformed churches in the Netherlands in 1562 and was revised by the Synod of Antwerp (1566) and the Synod of Dort (1618–1619). The following portion of the creed sets forth the content of the gospel. The reader should note that it contains all the doctrines of the gospel found in the Apostles' Creed and the Nicene Creed but in a far more developed form.

ARTICLE 18: We confess, therefore, that God has fulfilled the promise which He made to the fathers by the mouth of His holy prophets[1] when He sent into the world, at the time appointed by Him, His own only-begotten and eternal Son, "who took upon Him the form of a servant, and became like unto man,"[2] really assuming the true human nature, with all its infirmities, sin excepted,[3] being conceived in the womb of the blessed Virgin Mary, by the power of the Holy Spirit, without the means of man;[4] and did not only assume human nature as to the body, but also a true human soul,[5] that He might be a real man. For since the soul was lost as well as the body, it was necessary that He should take both upon Him, to save both....

1 Isa. 11:1; Luke 1:55; Gen. 26:4; 2 Sam. 7:12–16; Ps. 132:11;
Acts 13:23
2 1 Tim. 2:5; 3:16; Phil. 2:7
3 Heb. 2:14–15; 4:15
4 Luke 1:31, 34–35
5 Matt. 26:38; John 12:27

ARTICLE 20: We believe that God, who is perfectly merciful and just, sent His Son to assume that nature in which disobedience had been committed, to make satisfaction in the same and to bear the punishment of sin by His most bitter passion and death.[1] God therefore manifested His justice against His Son when He laid our iniquities on Him[2] and poured out His goodness and mercy on us, who were guilty and worthy of damnation, out of mere and perfect love, giving His Son unto death for us and raising Him for our justification,[3] that through Him we might obtain immortality and life eternal.

1 Heb. 2:14; Rom. 8:3, 32–33
2 Isa. 53:6; John 1:29; 1 John 4:9
3 Rom. 4:25

ARTICLE 21: We believe that Jesus Christ is ordained with an oath to be an everlasting High Priest after the order of Melchizedek,[1] and that He presented Himself in our behalf before the Father to appease His wrath by His full satisfaction,[2] by offering Himself on the tree of the cross, and pouring out His precious blood to purge away our sins, as the prophets had foretold. For it is written, "He was wounded for our transgressions, He was bruised for our iniquities: the chastisement of our peace was upon Him, and with His stripes we are healed. He was brought as a lamb to the slaughter and numbered with the transgressor";[3] and condemned by Pontius Pilate as a malefactor, though he had first declared Him innocent.[4] Therefore, "He restored that which He took not away,"[5] and "suffered the just for the unjust,"[6] as well in His body as in His soul, feeling the terrible punishment which our sins had merited; insomuch that "His sweat became like unto drops of blood falling down on the ground."[7] He called,

Community Aid

Thrift Store and Donation Center
4833 Carlisle Pike
Mechanicsburg, PA 17050
717-412-7706
www.communityaid.net

11/14/2024 11:55:42 AM   Jeremy

Hard Cover Book - $1.99	$1.99 Tx1
Student Discount 50%	($1.00)Tx1
Hard Cover Book - $1.99	$1.99 Tx1
Student Discount 50%	($1.00)Tx1

SUB TOTAL	$1.98
Sales Tax	$0.12

TOTAL	**$2.10**
Visa	$2.10

Item count: 2
Trans:57525   Terminal:050013029-001001

No Refunds or Exchanges

No Refunds or Exchanges

11/14/2024 11:55:42 AM   Jeremy
Trans:57525   Terminal:050013029-001001

TRANSACTION RECORD

Term#: 71770025023201
Loc#: 001   Reg#: POS1
Tran#: 57525
Term Id: Term1
Cashier: 382
CREDIT CARD PURCHASE
Batch: 5

                             Ref: 446
11-14-2024   11:56 AM
Card#: XXXXXXXXXXXXX4530
Card Type: VISA
Proximity
AID: A0000000031010
VISA DEBIT

                             Inv#: 446
                  Link#: 2430611560197
Auth#: 465240
Total: $2.10

        Retain this copy for your
                 records

         A0000 APPROVED

         Customer Copy

Trans:57525   Terminal:050013029-001001

No Refunds or Exchanges

"My God, My God, why hast Thou forsaken Me?" and hath
suffered all this for the remission of our sins.[8] Wherefore we
justly say, with the apostle Paul, "that we know nothing but
Jesus Christ and Him crucified,"[9] "we count all things but loss
and dung for the excellency of the knowledge of Christ Jesus
our Lord,"[10] in whose wounds we find all manner of consola-
tion. Neither is it necessary to seek or invent other means of
being reconciled to God than this only sacrifice, once offered,
by which believers are made perfect forever.[11]

[1] Ps. 110:4; Heb. 5:10
[2] Col. 1:14; Rom. 5:8–9; Col. 2:14; Heb. 2:17; 9:14; Rom. 3:24; 8:2;
     John 15:3; Acts 2:24; 13:28; John 3:16; 1 Tim. 2:6
[3] Isa. 53:5, 7, 12
[4] Luke 23:22, 24; Acts 13:28; Ps. 22:16; John 18:38; Ps. 69:5;
     1 Peter 3:18
[5] Ps. 69:4
[6] 1 Peter 3:18
[7] Luke 22:44
[8] Ps. 22:2; Matt. 27:46
[9] 1 Cor. 2:2
[10] Phil. 3:8
[11] Heb. 9:25–26; 10:14

The Westminster and 1689 London Baptist Confessions

In 1643, the English Parliament called on "learned, godly and judi-
cious" theologians and parliamentarians to gather at Westminster
Abbey in London in order to restructure the Church of England in
doctrine, practice, and worship. In 1646, as the result of these gather-
ings, the Westminster Confession of Faith was redacted and approved.
It was published a year later in 1647. In that same year it was adopted
as the subordinate standard (i.e., a standard that is subordinate to the
Scriptures) of the Church of Scotland. It is the prominent confession
of conservative Presbyterian churches throughout the world.

The 1689 London Baptist Confession is an adaptation of the
Westminster Confession of Faith made by the Particular Baptists
of England. Some of the modifications were made by the redactors
themselves, while others were taken from the First London Baptist
Confession of 1644 and the Savoy Declaration, which was published

by Congregationalist churches in 1658. The purpose of the 1689 Confession was to demonstrate the unity and continuity of the Christian faith that exists between the Particular Baptists and the Reformed faith in England and throughout the world.

In the following articles regarding the nature of the gospel, the Westminster and 1689 London Baptist Confessions are nearly identical. The following excerpt is taken from chapter 8 of the 1689 London Baptist Confession:

1. It pleased God, in His eternal purpose, to choose and ordain the Lord Jesus, His only begotten Son, according to the Covenant made between them both,[1] to be the Mediator between God and man, the Prophet,[2] Priest,[3] and King,[4] the Head and Savior of His Church,[5] the Heir of all things,[6] and Judge of the world:[7] unto whom He did from all eternity give a people, to be His seed[8] and to be by Him in time redeemed, called, justified, sanctified, and glorified.[9]

    [1] Isa. 42:1; 1 Peter 1:19–20; 1 Tim. 2:5
    [2] Acts 3:22
    [3] Heb. 5:5–6
    [4] Ps. 2:6; Luke 1:33
    [5] Eph. 5:23
    [6] Heb. 1:2
    [7] Acts 17:31
    [8] John 17:6; Ps. 22:30; Isa. 53:10
    [9] 1 Tim. 2:6; Isa. 55:4–5; 1 Cor. 1:30

2. The Son of God, the second person of the Holy Trinity, being very and eternal God, the brightness of the Father's glory, of one substance and equal with Him, who made the World, who upholdeth and governeth all things He hath made, did when the fullness of time was come, take upon Him man's nature,[10] with all the essential properties, and common infirmities thereof, yet without sin;[11] being conceived by the power of the Holy Spirit, in the womb of the virgin Mary, the Holy Spirit coming down upon her, and the power of the Most High overshadowing her, and so was made of a woman of the Tribe of Judah, of the Seed of Abraham, and David according to the Scriptures:[12] So that

two whole, perfect, and distinct natures were inseparably joined together in one person, without conversion, composition, or confusion.[13] Which person is very God, and very man, yet one Christ, the only Mediator between God and man.[14]

[10] John 1:1, 14; 1 John 5:20; Phil. 2:6; Gal. 4:4
[11] Heb. 2:14–17
[12] Luke 1:27, 31, 35; Gal. 4:4
[13] Luke 1:35; Col. 2:9; Rom. 9:5; 1 Peter 3:18; 1 Tim. 3:16
[14] Rom. 1:3–4; 1 Tim. 2:5

3. The Lord Jesus, in His human nature thus united to the divine, in the Person of the Son, was sanctified, and anointed with the Holy Spirit, above measure,[15] having in Him all the treasures of wisdom and knowledge;[16] in whom it pleased the Father that all fullness should dwell;[17] to the end that, being holy, harmless, undefiled, and full of grace and truth,[18] He might be thoroughly furnished to execute the office of a Mediator and Surety.[19] Which office He took not upon Himself, but was thereunto called by His Father,[20] who also put all power and judgment into His hand, and gave Him commandment to execute the same.[21]

[15] Ps. 45:7; John 3:34
[16] Col. 2:3
[17] Col. 1:19
[18] Heb. 7:26; John 1:14
[19] Acts 10:38; Heb. 12:24; 7:22
[20] Heb. 5:4–5
[21] John 5:22, 27; Matt. 28:18; Acts 2:36

4. This office the Lord Jesus did most willingly undertake;[22] which that He might discharge, He was made under the law,[23] and did perfectly fulfil it;[24] and underwent the punishment due to us, which we should have borne and suffered, being made sin and a curse for us: enduring most grievous sorrows in His soul,[25] and most painful sufferings in His body;[26] was crucified, and died,[27] and remained in the state of the dead; yet saw no corruption.[28] On the third day He arose from the dead,[29] with the same body in which He suffered,[30] with which also He ascended into

heaven, and there sits at the right hand of His Father,[31] making intercession,[32] and shall return, to judge men and angels, at the end of the world.[33]

[22] Ps. 40:7–8; Heb. 10:5–10; John 10:18; Phil. 2:8
[23] Gal. 4:4
[24] Matt. 3:15; 5:17
[25] Matt. 26:37–38; Luke 22:44; Matt. 27:46
[26] Matt. 26–27
[27] Phil. 2:8
[28] Acts 2:23–24, 27; 13:37; Rom. 6:9
[29] 1 Cor. 15:3–5
[30] John 20:25–27
[31] Mark 16:19
[32] Rom. 8:34; Heb. 9:24–25
[33] Rom. 14:9; Acts 1:11; 10:42; Matt. 13:40–42; Jude 6; 2 Peter 2:4

5. The Lord Jesus, by His perfect obedience, and sacrifice of Himself, which He through the eternal Spirit, once offered up unto God, has fully satisfied the justice of His God,[34] procured reconciliation, and purchased an everlasting inheritance in the kingdom of heaven, for those whom the Father has given unto Him.[35]

[34] Rom. 5:19; Heb. 9:14–16; 10:14; Eph. 5:2; Rom. 3:25–26
[35] Dan. 9:24–26; Col. 1:19–20; Eph. 1:11, 14; John 17:2; Heb. 9:12, 15

6. Although the price of redemption was not actually paid by Christ till after His incarnation, yet the virtue, efficacy, and benefits thereof were communicated to the elect, in all ages successively from the foundation of the world, in and by those promises, types, and sacrifices, wherein He was revealed, and signified to be the seed of the woman which should bruise the serpent's head; and the Lamb slain from the foundation of the world; being the same yesterday and today, and forever.[36]

[36] Gal. 4:4–5; Gen. 3:15; Rev. 13:8; Heb. 13:8

7. Christ, in the work of mediation, acteth according to both natures, by each nature doing that which is proper to itself;[37] yet, by reason of the unity of the person, that which is proper to one nature is sometimes in Scripture attributed to the person denominated by the other nature.[38]

[37] Heb. 9:14; 1 Peter 3:18
[38] Acts 20:28; John 3:13; 1 John 3:16

8. To all those for whom Christ hath obtained eternal redemption, He does certainly and effectually apply and communicate the same;[39] making intercession for them,[40] uniting them to Himself by His Spirit, revealing unto them, in and by the Word, the mystery of salvation;[41] effectually persuading them by His Spirit to believe and obey, and governing their hearts by His Word and Spirit;[42] overcoming all their enemies by His almighty power and wisdom, in such manner, and ways, as are most consonant to His wonderful and unsearchable dispensation;[43] and all of free, and absolute grace, without any condition foreseen in them, to procure it.

[39] John 6:37, 39; 10:15–16
[40] 1 John 2:1–2; Rom. 8:34
[41] John 15:13, 15; Eph. 1:7–9; John 17:6
[42] John 14:16; Heb. 12:2; 2 Cor. 4:13; Rom. 8:9, 14; 15:18–19; John 17:17
[43] Ps. 110:1; 1 Cor. 15:25–26; Mal. 4:2–3; Col. 2:15

Conclusion

These foundational creeds and confessions prove beyond a shadow of a doubt that the essential truths of the gospel of Jesus Christ have been preserved throughout the long history of the church. We know that we have nearly two millennia of Bible-believing Christians on our side whenever we proclaim Christ's deity, incarnation, perfect life, vicarious suffering, death, bodily resurrection, and exaltation to the right hand of God as Savior, Lord, and Judge of all. Through the grace and unassailable providence of God, this has been the central message of the church and will continue to be until the end of the age! It has been handed down to us as a sacred deposit and a solemn stewardship. We must study it, believe it, cherish it, proclaim it, guard it, and contend earnestly for it. Finally, we must hand it down to the next generation without subtraction, addition, or alteration.

5

THE PREEMINENCE
OF THE GOSPEL

In Colossians 1:18, the apostle Paul wrote the following about the person of Jesus Christ, "He is the head of the body, the church, who is the beginning, the firstborn from the dead, that in all things He may have the preeminence." The word *preeminence* is translated from the Greek verb *prōteúō*, which means "to be first, to hold the first rank or highest dignity, to have the preeminence."[1] The English adjective *preeminent* is derived from the Latin verb *praeeminere* (*prae* [before] + *eminere* [to stand out]). It denotes that which excels or surpasses all others in rank, dignity, worth, essentiality, or importance. All three of these qualities are descriptive of Christ and His gospel.

There is simply no way to exaggerate the centrality and preeminence of the gospel. It is not the only message in Christianity, but it is first in rank, dignity, and beauty. It does not supplant the other great truths of Scripture, but it is their cornerstone and the prism through which their true wisdom is revealed and comprehended. To put it plainly, there is no Christianity, no religious devotion, and no true spirituality apart from the person and work of Jesus Christ. His gospel is the greatest revelation of God to men and angels, it is the only means by which fallen humanity might be saved, and it is the great means by which the Christian is motivated and guided to true piety or godliness. It is the preeminence of Christ and His gospel that led John Newton to write the following stanza:

---

1. William Mounce and Rick D. Bennett Jr., *Mounce Concise Greek-English Dictionary of the New Testament*, s.v. "*prōteúō*," Accordance Bible Software, 1993.

"What think ye of Christ?" is the test
To try both your state and your scheme;
You cannot be right in the rest
Unless you think rightly of Him.[2]

What do you think of Christ and His gospel? How you and I answer this question will tell all that needs to be told about us. However, we must always remember that our actions are what validate our confession. If Christ and His gospel are preeminent in our mind and heart, then He will certainly be preeminent in our proclamation, He will be the preeminent standard to which we seek to be conformed, and He will be the preeminent motivation of our life. In other words, if all is taken from us but this one thing, "Christ died for my sins," we would still have our message, our goal, our motivation, and our heart's desire!

In these next chapters, we will consider several specific matters of Christian faith and doctrine in which the gospel of Jesus Christ has preeminence: revelation, salvation, sanctification, study, and proclamation. The reader should remember that our consideration of these topics will by no means be exhaustive; it is cursory at best. An exhaustive or thorough study of any one of these themes could not be contained even in several volumes. This is one of the great problems and inevitable sorrows whenever we study even the most minute aspect of the gospel—it is infinite! It is worthy not merely of a lifetime but of an eternity of study.

As we begin to examine the Scriptures in this book, I pray that our spark might be fanned into a flame and our interest to know Christ might be transformed into an all-controlling passion. The goal is that, by the grace of God and the Spirit's supply, we may all be able to confess with the apostle Paul,

For the love of Christ compels us, because we judge thus: that if One died for all, then all died; and He died for all, that those

---

2. John Newton, *Olney Hymns* (London: W. Oliver, 1779), book 1, number 89.

who live should live no longer for themselves, but for Him who died for them and rose again. (2 Cor. 5:14–15)

But what things were gain to me, these I have counted loss for Christ. Yet indeed I also count all things loss for the excellence of the knowledge of Christ Jesus my Lord. (Phil. 3:7–8)

Before we begin, let us lift our voices in prayer to God with the same passion and petition of the eighteenth-century English nonconformist pastor, hymn writer, and educator Philip Doddridge:

Oh impress this gospel upon my soul, till its saving virtue be diffused over every faculty! Let it not only be heard, and acknowledged, and professed, but felt! Make it "thy power to my eternal salvation" [Rom. 1:16]; and raise me to that humble, tender gratitude, to that active, unwearied zeal in Thy service, which becomes one "to whom so much is forgiven" [Luke 7:47] and forgiven upon such terms as these.[3]

---

3. Philip Doddridge, *Rise and Progress of Religion in the Soul* (New York: American Tract Society, 1849), 120.

6

THE PREEMINENT REVELATION OF GOD

The word *revelation* is derived from the Latin verb *revelare* (*re* [again, in the sense of a reversal of something] + *velum* [veil]). It means literally to unveil something that was hidden. In the Greek New Testament, the word *reveal* is translated from the verb *apokalúptō* (*apó* [a reversal] + *kalúptō* [to cover]). It means to uncover or unveil. The revelation of God is a running or opening of the curtain, a disclosure of what was hidden, a manifestation of God's nature and will. Since God is infinitely valuable above all other persons and things combined, His revelation of Himself to man is *the* greatest gift that He can give and *the* greatest grace that He can bestow. Consequently, His concealment, His determination to hide Himself from man, is the greatest judgment.

The Scriptures teach that God has revealed Himself to man in many ways. First, there is a general revelation that has gone out to all humankind in every generation through creation and the law that has been written on the heart of every man. The apostle Paul affirmed this in the first two chapters of his epistle to the Romans:

> For since the creation of the world His invisible attributes are clearly seen, being understood by the things that are made, even His eternal power and Godhead, so that they are without excuse. (1:20)

> For when Gentiles, who do not have the law, by nature do the things in the law, these, although not having the law, are a law to themselves, who show the work of the law written in their hearts, their conscience also bearing witness, and between

themselves their thoughts accusing or else excusing them.
(2:14–15)

Beyond this general revelation, the Scriptures also testify that
God has granted specific revelation to humanity through His sovereign election of the nation of Israel. To this one people was entrusted
the very "oracles of God" (Rom. 3:2), that they might "know His will,
and approve the things that are excellent, being instructed out of the
law." In turn, they were to be "a guide to the blind, a light to those
who are in darkness, an instructor of the foolish, a teacher of babes,
having the form of knowledge and truth" (Rom. 2:18–20). However,
in spite of these great privileges, the nation of Israel did little better
than the Gentile or pagan nations that surrounded it. Consequently,
the world was all but consumed in spiritual darkness, idolatry, and
gross immorality (Eph. 4:17–19).

Yet when the world's stage was at its darkest, "when the fullness
of the time had come, God sent forth His Son" (Gal. 4:4) as "a light to
bring revelation to the Gentiles, and the glory of Your people Israel"
(Luke 2:32), that He might bring "salvation to the ends of the earth"
(Acts 13:47). It is the testimony of the Scriptures and every confession, creed, and catechism of the church that the incarnate Son
and His gospel is the greatest revelation of God to men and angels
and that the climax of that revelation is the cross of Calvary! It is
there that we find the most complete revelation of all of God's attributes in perfect harmony. There, His holiness and righteousness are
revealed in the just punishment of sin. There, His grace and mercy
are revealed in the suffering and death of His Son in the place of
His guilty people. Yes, it is at the cross that we behold the greatest revelation of the person and attributes of God, and it is through
the proclamation of this singular event that God continues to make
Himself known. When John wrote, "No one has seen God at any
time. The only begotten Son, who is in the bosom of the Father, He
has declared Him" (John 1:18), he was referring not only to Christ's
presence, teaching, and miracles but also to His cross. It is there that
we find the greatest explanation or exposition of God! As Edward
Payson wrote,

The gospel contains a grand display of the moral excellencies and perfections of Jehovah.... Suffice it to say, that here the moral character of Jehovah shines full-orbed and complete: here all the fullness of the Godhead, all the insufferable splendors of Deity, burst at once upon our aching sight: here the manifold perfections of God, holiness and goodness, justice and mercy, truth and grace, majesty and condescension, hatred of sin and compassion for sinners, are harmoniously blended, like the parti-colored (i.e. multi-colored) rays of solar light in one pure blaze of dazzling whiteness. Here, rather than on any of His other works, He founds His claims to the highest admiration, gratitude and love of His creatures:—here is the work, which ever has called forth, and which through eternity will continue to call forth the most rapturous praises of the celestial choirs, and feed the ever glowing fires of devotion in their breasts; for the glory which shines in the gospel is the glory which illuminates heaven, and the Lamb that was slain is the light thereof.[1]

Octavius Winslow, in *The Precious Things of God*, also spoke of the marvels to be found in studying the glory of Christ:

Oh, do not study God in the jeweled heavens—in the sublimity of the mountain—in the beauty of the valley—in the grandeur of the ocean—in the murmurs of the stream—in the music of the winds. God made all this, but all this is not God. Study Him in the cross of Jesus! Look at Him through this wondrous telescope, and although, as through a glass darkly, you behold His glory—the Godhead in awful eclipse, the Sun of His Deity setting in blood—yet that rude and crimsoned cross more fully reveals the mind of God, more harmoniously discloses the perfections of God, and more perfectly unveils the heart of God, and more fully exhibits the glory of God, than the combined power of ten thousand worlds like this, even though sin had never marred, and the curse had never

---

1. Edward Payson, *The Complete Works of Edward Payson* (Harrisonburg, Va.: Sprinkle Publications, 1998), 3:42–43.

blighted it. Study God in Christ, and Christ on the cross! Oh, the marvels that meet in it—the glory that gathers round it—the streams of blessing that flow from it—the deep refreshing shadow it casts, in the happy experience of all who look to Jesus and live—who look to Jesus and love—who look to Jesus and obey—who look to Jesus and embrace that blessed "hope of eternal life which God, who cannot lie, promised before the world began." A worthy structure this of a foundation so divine![2]

---

2. Octavius Winslow, *The Precious Things of God* (Louisville, Ky.: GLH Publishing, 2015), 7–8.

7

THE PREEMINENT
MESSAGE OF SALVATION

The word *salvation* is derived from the Greek noun *sotēría*, which may refer to a physical or spiritual rescue or deliverance. Spiritually, it refers to a sovereign act that God initiates and consummates and by which He delivers His people from the consequences and power of sin and restores them to a reconciled relationship with Himself. This is accomplished ultimately through the gospel of Jesus Christ.

Throughout the Old and New Testaments, God is revealed as the Savior or Redeemer of His people (Ps. 17:7; Isa. 60:16; Titus 3:4; 1 Tim. 2:3). In fact, the Scriptures declare salvation to be God's royal prerogative—a right He shares with no one. The psalmist cried out, "Salvation belongs to the LORD" (Ps. 3:8) and again, "The salvation of the righteous is from the LORD" (37:39). The prophet Jonah affirmed the same when, from the belly of a great fish, he confessed, "Salvation is of the LORD" (Jonah 2:9). Speaking through the prophet Isaiah, God is even more explicit: "I, even I, am the LORD, and besides Me there is no savior" (Isa. 43:11) and "There is no other God besides Me, a just God and a Savior; there is none besides Me" (45:21). For this reason, the Lord calls all peoples, regardless of their nationality or cultural identification, to turn to Him for salvation: "Look to Me, and be saved, all you ends of the earth! For I am God, and there *is* no other" (Isa. 45:22).

The fact that God will not share the title of savior with another tells us a great deal about the person of Jesus Christ. Throughout the New Testament, He is repeatedly called Savior (Luke 1:69; John 4:42; Acts 5:31; Rom. 11:26; Titus 3:6; 1 John 4:14), and the work of saving is consistently attributed to Him (Matt. 1:21; Luke 19:10; Acts 15:11; 16:31; Rom. 10:9; 1 Thess. 5:9; 1 Tim. 1:15), even to the exclusion of all others (Acts 4:12; 1 Tim. 2:5; 1 John 5:11–12). Peter's affirmation in Acts 4:12 is especially significant: "Nor is there salvation in any other, for there is no other name under heaven given among men by which we must be saved." For Peter to attribute salvation exclusively to the name of Christ leaves us with only one possible conclusion— He is God in the most complete sense of the term!

The difficulty of accomplishing the eternal salvation of fallen and morally corrupt humanity should never be underestimated. Jesus affirms that it would be easier for a camel to go through the eye of a needle than for a sinner (rich or poor) to enter the kingdom of God (Matt. 19:23–26). The difficulty is due not only to our moral corruption and sin but also to God's holy and righteous nature. If God were amoral or immoral, our sin would not present a problem, but since He loves righteousness and hates all unrighteousness, our sin presents the greatest dilemma: How can God pardon sin without contradicting His holy and righteous nature? Or, borrowing from the language of the apostle Paul in Romans 3:26, how can God be just and the justifier of the wicked? The answer to this greatest of all questions is found in the gospel of Jesus Christ. The Son of God became a true man and lived a life of perfect obedience to the law of God. On Calvary He bore the sin of His people, suffered the wrath of God that was due them, and satisfied the demands of God's justice that were contrary to them. Thus, Jesus made it possible for the Father to forgive His sinful people without the least violation of His righteousness and to call them to Himself without the least offense to His holiness. This is not just *a message* among many; it is *the message* above all others. The "word of the cross" is the word of the church. It is to be center in our hearts, foremost in our thoughts, and the beginning and ending of all our preaching. It is this message that sets Christianity apart from all other religions. It gives the church her life, her strength, and her beauty. To lose this message, dilute it, or treat it as secondary in importance is to drive a dagger through the very heart of our faith. If only one truth is gleaned from these pages, let it be that the gospel is the most preeminent theme of biblical, reformed, and evangelical Christianity. As Matthew Henry wrote, "The doctrine of Christ's death and resurrection is at the foundation of Christianity. Remove this foundation, and the whole fabric falls, all our hopes for eternity sink at once. And it is by holding this truth firmly that Christians are made to stand in a day of trial, and kept faithful to God."[1]

R. C. H. Lenski also warned of the danger of diminishing the gospel of Christ:

> In all the universe there is no other power that can save as much as a single soul. To reject the gospel is thus to reject salvation. To substitute something in place of the gospel is to substitute the loss of salvation for salvation. To dilute or alter the gospel is to reduce its power, possibly to a point where its power can no longer save.... The gospel is God's power to effect salvation. The danger implied is the destructive, damning power of sin and death, Satan and his kingdom of darkness and doom. What human power is able to effect an escape from that? The security implied is that of pardon, peace, union with Christ and God in the kingdom of heaven as sons of God, children of light, heirs of heaven. What human power is able to achieve these?[2]

Finally, Samuel Davies underscores just how essential it is to come to a saving knowledge of Jesus Christ:

> When I consider I am speaking to an assembly of sinners, guilty, depraved, helpless creatures, and that, if ever you be saved, it will be only through Jesus Christ, in that way which the gospel reveals; when I consider that your everlasting life and happiness turn upon this hinge, namely, the reception you give to this Saviour, and this way of salvation; I say, when

1. Matthew Henry, *Matthew Henry's Commentary* (Mclean, Va.: MacDonald Publishing, 1980), 6:585.
2. R. C. H. Lenski, *The Interpretation of Saint Paul's Epistle to the Romans* (Minneapolis, Minn.: Augsburg Publishing, 1961), 74–75.

I consider these things, I can think of no subject I can more properly choose than to recommend the Lord Jesus to your acceptance, and to explain and inculcate (i.e. instill, implant, impress) the method of salvation through His mediation; or, in other words, to preach the pure gospel to you; for the gospel, in the most proper sense, is nothing else but a revelation of a way of salvation for sinners of Adam's race.[3]

---

3. Samuel Davies, *The Sermons of Rev. Samuel Davies* (Morgan, Pa.: Soli Deo Gloria, 1997), 1:109.

8

THE PREEMINENT MEANS
OF SANCTIFICATION

The gospel is well recognized as the preeminent message of salvation, but oftentimes its preeminence in the work of sanctification is overlooked or even discounted. Nevertheless, a close examination of the Scriptures will prove that the gospel is truly the power of God for salvation to everyone who believes (Rom. 1:16), with regard to not only our justification but also our sanctification. A first look of faith at the gospel saves us, but an ongoing look at the gospel will transform us and conform us in increasing measure to the image of Jesus Christ. As the apostle Paul wrote to the church in Corinth, "But we all, with unveiled face, beholding as in a mirror the glory of the Lord, are being transformed into the same image from glory to glory, just as by the Spirit of the Lord" (2 Cor. 3:18). It is for this reason that George Whitefield pleaded,

> O ye believers, my heart is enlarged towards you. Look to, and live much on the blessed Jesus, and then you will live to, and act for Him more and more. Be thankful for what you have received, but be looking out continually for fresh discoveries of His love, and fresh incomes of heavenly grace, till you are called to behold this Lamb of God in glory.[1]

The transformative power of the gospel not only informs the mind but also moves the heart. Oftentimes our motivation falls far behind our knowledge so that we find it difficult to keep pace or

---

1. George Whitefield, *The Sermons of George Whitefield* (Wheaton, Ill.: Crossway, 2012), 2:421.

walk according to the commands we know. But the gospel works on the heart, draws out our affections for God, and moves us to obedience. The more we comprehend of God's redemptive work on our behalf, the more kindled our passion and the more likely our devotion will burst into flame. The great saints of church history were not of any better stock than the rest of us, for all believers are born with the same moral corruption and all are renewed by the same Spirit. The great distance between their exceptional devotion and ours is simply a greater knowledge of the gospel of Jesus Christ. The more we know of what He has done and has accomplished on our behalf, the more we will be both motivated and transformed. The apostle Paul affirmed this in 2 Corinthians 5:14–15: "For the love of Christ compels us, because we judge thus: that if One died for all, then all died; and He died for all, that those who live should live no longer for themselves, but for Him who died for them and rose again."

It was the love of Christ revealed through the gospel that made the apostle Paul a most eminent servant of God. This truth has been affirmed over and over throughout the history of the church. For example, John Calvin wrote, "The more extraordinary the discoveries which have reached us of the Redeemer's kindness, the more strongly are we bound to His service."[2] And George Whitefield also asserted, "The death of Jesus Christ has turned our whole lives into one continued sacrifice. And whether we eat or drink, whether we pray to God, or do anything to man, it must all be done out of a love for and knowledge of Him who died and rose again, to render all, even our most ordinary deeds, acceptable in the sight of God."[3]

This emphasis on the gospel as the great means of sanctification is not meant to deny or diminish the place of God's commandments in the Christian life. The psalmist's declaration regarding the law's usefulness in our sanctification remains intact: "Through Your precepts I get understanding; therefore I hate every false way. Your word

---

2. John Calvin, *Calvin's Commentaries* (Grand Rapids, Mich.: Baker, 1979), 21:304.

3. Whitefield, *Sermons of George Whitefield*, 2:237.

is a lamp to my feet and a light to my path. I have sworn and confirmed that I will keep Your righteous judgments" (Ps. 119:104–6).

The true intent of the law that Christ honored, the commands and precepts that He taught during His earthly ministry, and the instruction that He gave us through the inspired writers of the New Testament are an exceedingly great treasure and infallible guide. Through them we understand both the character of God and the way in which we should walk. However, in the cross we find our great motivation to give ourselves fully to God and His will. We have been given many worthy reasons to live in relentless devotion to God—creation, providence, common grace, and an infinite number of other kindnesses. Nevertheless, the cross of Christ stands above them all, as Edward Payson noted:

> In his epistles to the Corinthians, St. Paul informs us that he determined to know or make known, nothing but Jesus Christ and him crucified [1 Cor. 2:2]. Did he then intend so to confine himself to the doctrines of the cross, as to say nothing, in his preaching, of moral duties? By no means. All his epistles prove that he did not. But he intended to illustrate and enforce moral duties in an evangelical manner, by motives and illustrations derived from the cross of Christ.[4]

Charles Simeon also wrote on the importance of seeking and relying on Christ as it relates to our obedience to God:

> There were two particular views in which Paul invariably spoke of the death of Christ; namely, as the ground of our hopes, and as the motive to our obedience.... Strongly as he enforced the necessity of relying on Christ, and founding our hopes of salvation solely on His obedience unto death, he was no less earnest in promoting the interests of holiness. Whilst he represented the believers as "dead to the law" and "without law," he still insisted that they were "under the law to Christ," and as much bound to obey every tittle of it as ever

---

4. Payson, *Complete Works of Edward Payson*, 3:136.

[1 Cor. 9:21; Gal. 2:19]: and he enforced obedience to it, in all its branches, and to the utmost possible extent. Moreover, when the doctrines which he had inculcated (i.e. instilled) were in danger of being abused to licentious purposes, he expressed his utter abhorrence of such a procedure [Rom. 6:1, 15]; and declared, that "the grace of God, which brought salvation, taught them, that denying ungodliness and worldly lusts, they should live righteously, soberly, and godly in this present world" [Titus 2:11–12]. A life of holy obedience is represented by him as the great object which Christ aimed to produce in all His people: indeed the very name, Jesus, proclaimed, that the object of His coming was "to save his people from their sins" [Matt. 1:21]. The same was the scope and end of His death, even to "redeem them from all iniquity, and to purify unto himself a peculiar people zealous of good works" [Titus 2:14]. His resurrection and ascension to heaven had also the same end in view; for "therefore he both died, and rose, and revived, that he might be the Lord both of the dead and living" [Rom. 14:9]. Impressed with a sense of these things himself, St. Paul laboured more abundantly than any of the Apostles in his holy vocation: he proceeded with a zeal which nothing could quench, and an ardour which nothing could damp: privations, labours, imprisonments, deaths, were of no account in his eyes; "none of these things moved him, neither counted he his life dear unto him, so that he might but finish his course with joy, and fulfil the ministry that was committed to him" [Acts 20:24]. But what was the principle by which he was actuated? He himself tells us, that he was impelled by a sense of obligation to Christ, for all that He had done and suffered for him: "the love of Christ constraineth us," says he; "because we thus judge, that if one died for all, then were all dead; and that He died for all, that they who live should not henceforth live unto themselves, but unto Him who died for them and rose again" [2 Cor. 5:14–15]. This is that principle which he desired to be universally embraced, and endeavoured to impress on the minds of all: "We beseech you, brethren," says he, "by the mercies of God, that you present your bodies a living sacrifice, holy, acceptable to God, which is your reasonable service" [Rom. 12:1]. What mercies he refers to, we are at no loss to determine; they are the great mercies vouchsafed to us in the work of redemption: for so he says in another place; "Ye are bought with a price; therefore glorify God in your body and in your spirit, which are his" [1 Cor. 6:19–20]. Now this is the subject which the Apostle comprehends under the term "Christ crucified." It consists of two parts: First, of affiance (i.e. trust) in Christ for salvation, and, next, of obedience to the law for His sake: had either part of it been taken alone, his views had been imperfect, and his ministry without success. Had he neglected to set forth Christ as the only Saviour of the world, he would have betrayed his trust, and led his hearers to build their hopes on a foundation of sand. On the other hand, if he had neglected to inculcate (i.e. instill) holiness, and to set forth redeeming love as the great incentive to obedience, he would have been justly chargeable with that which has been often falsely imputed to him,—an antinomian spirit; and his doctrines would have merited the odium which has most unjustly been cast upon them. But on neither side did he err: he forgot neither the foundation nor the superstructure: he distinguished properly between them, and kept each in its place.[5]

The sanctifying power of the gospel should be both an encouragement and a call to self-examination. We should be encouraged to know that the more we truly comprehend the truths of the gospel, the more we will be impassioned and transformed by them. However, we should also sincerely examine ourselves to determine if our knowledge has led to transformation. True knowledge of the gospel is not measured by the number of facts that we have accumulated about the gospel of Christ, but by our conformity to the Christ of the gospel. Like all theology, true gospel study is a devotion, an act of worship, resulting in transformation. John Owen made this point very well:

---

5. Charles Simeon, *Expository Outlines on the Whole Bible* (Grand Rapids, Mich.: Baker, 1988), 16:35, 37–39.

Knowledge of political theory is not the same as statesman-
ship, nor does a keen study of Cicero's Laws and Plato's
Republic automatically produce good citizens. By the same
reasoning, a Christian theologian is not a man with some
superficial knowledge or slight grasp of a technical scheme of
theology and its scientific terminology. If he bears no mark of
a true disciple of Christ, then he is no theologian, but rather
remains a miserable sinner, standing self-condemned. Such
scholars were well described long since by Philostratus, "If
what we teach is contradicted by our own behavior, then we
are shown to have been speaking in an unnatural manner,
merely making sounds like a flute player."…

Let us proclaim it boldly—the man who is not inflamed
with divine love is an outsider to all theology! Let him toil
long and hard in the arming of thorny questions; let him be
the most avid devourer of theological books in existence; if he
has this and nothing else, it is but the stronger proof that the
natural beauty of God's truth has never penetrated through
even the smallest chink into his mind. He is not on fire with
love of divine truth, nor carried away with admiration of her
beauty.[6]

John Owen's exhortation can be applied to all categories of theological thought, but how much more to the gospel—the acropolis of
all theology? Let us study with earnest longing and many prayers to
know Christ and be transformed by His gospel! And let us measure
our knowledge of the gospel by the transformation it has wrought in
our lives.

---

6. Owen, *Biblical Theology*, 619, xlvi.

9

THE PREEMINENT
SUBJECT OF STUDY

The life of man is of such short duration and yet there exist so many worthy subjects of study—language, literature, history, mathematics, and the nearly innumerable categories of science. If every human of the billions who dwell on this planet possessed an intellect of the highest genius, and all dedicated themselves to a singular discipline of science, they would still not be able to exhaust all that is to be known about that one subject.

What a marvelous universe God has created! Yet of all the worthy subjects of investigation and contemplation, one rises above them all like an Everest above the smallest mound. It is the knowledge of God revealed in the gospel of Jesus Christ. Charles Simeon explained,

> Of all the subjects that can occupy the human mind, there is not one so great and glorious as that of redemption through the incarnation and death of God's only-begotten Son. It is that which occupies incessantly the heavenly hosts; and which the Apostle Paul, whatever be his more immediate subject of discourse, reverts to on every occasion: and when he has, however incidentally, touched upon it, he scarcely knows how, or when, to leave it.[1]

William Bates likewise marveled at the unfathomable depths of Scripture:

---

1. Simeon, *Expository Outlines*, 18:166.

The Apostle tells us that the mystery of our redemption contains all the "treasures of wisdom and knowledge" [Col. 2:3] to signify their excellence and abundance: the "unsearchable riches" of grace are laid up in it. There is infinite variety, and perpetual matter for the inquiry of the most excellent understanding. No created reason is able to reach its height or sound its depths. By the continual study, and increase in the knowledge of it, the mind enjoys a persevering pleasure, that far exceeds the short vehemence of sensual delights.[2]

Isaac Ambrose, in *Looking unto Jesus*, also considered how sweet the never-ending study of Christ can be:

I may feelingly say, [Christ] is the sweetest subject that ever was preached on. Is it not "as an ointment poured forth," whose smell is so fragrant, and whose savor is so sweet, that "therefore all the virgins love him?" Is it not comprehensive of all glory, beauty, excellency, whether of things in heaven or of things on earth? Is it not a mystery, sweet and deep? Surely volumes are written of Jesus Christ: there is line upon line, sermon upon sermon, book upon book, and tome upon tome, and yet such is the mystery, that we are all but, as yet, at the first side of the single Catechism of Jesus Christ: yea.... It is a worthy study to make farther and farther discovery of this blessed mystery; and it were to be wished that all the ministers of Christ would spend themselves in the spelling, and reading, and understanding of it.[3]

There was a time in academia when theology was considered the "queen of the sciences," but now the greater part of mankind no longer considers it even worthy of honorable mention. This is to be expected by a fallen world that is at enmity with God (John 3:19–20; Rom. 8:7), but it is a great surprise and a cause for fierce lament when such an attitude of apathy and neglect is found among God's people,

---

2. Bates, *Harmony of the Divine Attributes*, 104.
3. Ambrose, *Looking unto Jesus*, viii.

even among His ministers. Will we pass over diamonds to play with marbles? Will we shun gold to gather stones?

In the hands of a wise and noble teacher, "art appreciation" is a worthy discipline designed to refine and redirect the student's interest and affection from that which is base or common to that which is truly worthy of delight, contemplation, and conversation and possesses the capacity to transform, elevate, and satisfy both mind and soul. Today, the church and individual Christians need instruction in "theological appreciation," especially regarding the gospel. Believers' interests and affections need to be refined and redirected not merely from the bad to the good but also from the good to the most excellent—the revelation of God in the person and work of Jesus Christ. As Thomas Goodwin wrote, "There is not a truth of the gospel, but it is more worth than gold, more rich than precious stones."[4]

A church that is fed only on principles and commands will languish from malnutrition. Its heart will wither, its hope will fade, and its vitality will be drained. But a church fed on Christ and His gospel will go from strength to strength and from glory to glory, for "the people who know their God shall be strong" (Dan. 11:32). The believer must make the study of Christ and His gospel a life discipline, and the minister must consider it to be his greatest stewardship. In fact, the minister is to be a teacher of "theological appreciation." He must spend long hours each day mining the great gems of Christ from the Scriptures so that he might present them to God's people with every opportunity. The goal of all his endeavors must be that God's people might turn their interests and affections to God; that they might refuse the fodder of the world because they have tasted and seen that the Lord is good (Ps. 34:8); and that their mind might be elevated, their affections refined, their character transformed, and their souls completely satisfied in Christ and His gospel.

Although the most disciplined among us will never reach the level of devotion that the gospel deserves, we must attempt to give

---

4. Thomas Goodwin, *The Works of Thomas Goodwin, D.D.* (Grand Rapids: Reformation Heritage Books, 2022), 4:307.

our all. Although the most insightful of us will end our days far short of knowing all that is to be known about Christ and His gospel, it is still the most worthy endeavor to which we could ever aspire. Although the goal we have set for ourselves will not be attained even after an eternity of eternities, the transformation of the soul will be immeasurable! John Flavel clearly felt the same:

> Oh then study Christ, study to know him more extensively. There be many excellent things in Christ, that the most eagle-eyed believer hath not yet seen: Ah! 'tis pity that any thing of Christ should be hid from His people. Study to know Christ more intensively, to get the experimental taste and lively power of His knowledge upon your hearts and affections: This is the knowledge that carries all the sweetness and comfort in it.[5]

Charles Spurgeon likewise underscored the immense value of devoted study of Jesus Christ:

> Study Christ; the most excellent of all the sciences is the knowledge of a crucified Savior. He is most learned in the university of heaven who knows most of Christ. He who hath known most of Him still says that His love surpasseth knowledge. Behold Him, then, with wonder, and behold Him with thankfulness.[6]

> Jesus Christ, as the atoning sacrifice, ought to be the principal object of every believer's thoughts. There are other subjects in the world which we must think of, for we are yet in the body; but this one subject ought to engross our souls, and, as the birds fly to their nests so ought we, whenever our minds are let loose, to fly back to Jesus Christ. He should be the main topic of each day's consideration and of each night's reflection. We might, with truthfulness, transfer the words of the first psalm, and say,

---

5. Flavel, *Works of John Flavel*, 1:39.
6. Charles Spurgeon, *Metropolitan Tabernacle Pulpit* (Pasadena, Tex.: Pilgrim Publications, 1975), 39:482.

"Blessed is the man whose delight is in the Christ of God and who meditates in Him both day and night; for he shall be as a tree planted by the rivers of water, that bringeth forth his fruit in his season; his leaf also shall not wither, and whatsoever he doeth shall prosper."

To meditate much upon the Lamb of God, is to occupy your minds with the grandest subject of thought in the universe. All others are flat compared with Him! What are the sciences but human ignorance set forth in order? What are the classics but the choicest of Babel's jargon when compared with His teachings? What are the poets but dreamers, and philosophers but fools in His presence? Jesus alone is wisdom, beauty, eloquence and power. No theme for contemplation can at all equal this noblest of all topics—God allied to human nature, God the Infinite, incarnate among sons of men, God in union with humanity taking human sin, out of love stupendous condescending to be numbered with the transgressors, and to suffer for sin that was not His own? O wonder and romance, if men desire ye, they may find you here! O love, if men seek thee, here alone, they may behold thee! O wisdom, if men dig for thee, here shall they discover thy purest ore! O happiness, if men pine for thee, thou dwellest with the Christ of God, and they enjoy thee who live in Him. O Lord Jesus, thou art all we need!

"Such as find Thee find such sweetness, deep, mysterious and unknown; Far above all worldly pleasures, if they were to meet in one."

Ye may search the heavens above and the earth beneath; ye may penetrate the secret mysteries to find out the first principles and the beginnings of things, but ye shall find more in the man of Nazareth, the equal with God, than in all else besides. He is the sum and substance of all truth, the essence of all creation, the soul of life; the light of light, the heaven of heavens, and yet He is greater far than all this, or all else that I could utter. There is no subject in the world so vast, so sublime, so pure, so elevating, so divine; give me to behold the Lord Jesus, and my eye seeth every precious thing.[7]

Stephen Charnock, in *The Existence and Attributes of God*, also extolled the pursuit of growing in the knowledge of Christ:

Study and admire the wisdom of God in redemption. This is the duty of all Christians. We are not called to understand the great depth of philosophy; we are not called to a skill in the intricacies of civil government, or understand all the methods of physic; but we are called to be Christians, that is, studiers of Divine evangelical wisdom. There are first principles to be learned; but not those principles to be rested in without a further progress: "Therefore, leaving the principles of the doctrine of Christ, let us go on to perfection" [Heb. 6:1]. Duties must be practiced, but knowledge is not to be neglected. The study of Gospel mysteries, the harmony of Divine truths, the sparkling of Divine wisdom, in their mutual combination to the great ends of God's glory and man's salvation, is an incentive to duty, a spur to worship, and particularly to the greatest and highest part of worship, that part which shall remain in heaven; the admiration and praise of God, and delight in Him. If we acquaint not ourselves with the impressions of the glory of Divine wisdom in it, we shall not much regard it as worthy our observance in regard of that duty. The gospel is a mystery; and, as a mystery, hath something great and magnificent in it worthy of our daily inspection; we shall find fresh springs of new wonders, which we shall be invited to adore with a religious astonishment. It will both raise and satisfy our longings. Who can come to the depths of "God manifested in the flesh?" How amazing is it, and unworthy of a slight thought, that the death of the Son of God should purchase the happy immortality of a sinful creature, and the glory of a rebel be wrought by the ignominy of so great a person! that our Mediator should have a nature whereby to covenant with His Father, and a nature whereby to be a

---

7. Spurgeon, *Metropolitan Tabernacle Pulpit*, 18:391–92.

Surety for the creature! How admirable is it, that the fallen creature should receive an advantage by the forfeiture of His happiness! How mysterious is it, that the Son of God should bow down to death upon a cross for the satisfaction of justice; and rise triumphantly out of the grave, as a declaration, that justice was contented and satisfied! that He should be exalted to heaven to intercede for us; and at last return into the world to receive us, and invest us with a glory forever with Himself! Are these things worthy of a careless regard, or a blockish amazement? What understanding can pierce into the depths of the divine doctrine of the incarnation and birth of Christ; the indissoluble union of the two natures? What capacity is able to measure the miracles of that wisdom, found in the whole draught and scheme of the gospel? Doth it not merit, then, to be the object of our daily meditation? How comes it to pass, then, that we are so little curious to concern our thoughts in those wonders, that we scarce taste or sip of these delicacies? that we busy ourselves in trifles, and consider what we shall eat, and in what fashion we shall be dressed; please ourselves with the ingeniousness of a lace or feather; admire a motheaten manuscript, or some half-worn piece of antiquity, and think our time ill-spent in the contemplating and celebrating that wherein God hath busied Himself, and eternity is designed for the perpetual expressions of? How inquisitive are the blessed angels! with what vigor do they renew their daily contemplations of it, and receive a fresh contentment from it; still learning, and still inquiring [1 Peter 1:12]! Their eye is never off the mercyseat; they strive to see the bottom of it, and employ all the understanding they have to conceive the wonders of it. Shall the angels be ravished with it, and bend themselves down to study it, who have but little interest in it in comparison of us, for whom it was both contrived and dispensed;—and shall not our pains be greater for this hidden treasure? Is not that worthy the study of a rational creature, that is worthy the study of the angelical? There must indeed be pains; it is expressed by "digging" [Prov. 2:4]. A lazy arm will not sink to the depth of a mine. The neglect of meditating on it is inexcusable, since it hath the title and character of the wisdom of God. The ancient prophets searched into it, when it was folded up in shadows, when they saw only the fringes of Wisdom's garment [1 Peter 1:10]; and shall not we, since the sun hath mounted up in our horizon, and sensibly scattered the light of the knowledge of this and the other perfections of God? As the Jewish sabbath was appointed to celebrate the perfections of God, discovered in creation, so is the Christian sabbath appointed to meditate on, and bless God, for the discovery of his perfections in redemption. Let us, therefore, receive it according to its worth: let it be our only rule to walk by. It is worthy to be valued above all other counsels; and we should never think of it without the doxology of the apostle, "To the only wise God be glory through Jesus Christ, for ever!" that our speculations may end in affectionate admirations, and thanksgivings, for that which is so full of wonders. What a little prospect should we have had of God, and the happiness of man, had not his wisdom and goodness revealed these things to us! The gospel is a marvelous light, and should not be regarded with a stupid ignorance, and pursued with a duller practice.[8]

8. Stephen Charnock, *The Existence and Attributes of God* (Grand Rapids, Mich.: Baker, 1997), 1:598–600.

10

THE PREEMINENT
SUBJECT OF PREACHING

The gospel is most certainly to be believed, studied, and exemplified
in our lives, yet the great emphasis in the New Testament is on proclaiming it. At the very beginning of His earthly ministry, "Jesus came
to Galilee, preaching the gospel of the kingdom of God" (Mark 1:14).
At the end of His ministry, He commanded His disciples, "Go into all
the world and preach the gospel to every creature" (Mark 16:15).

The book of Acts bears abundant testimony that the apostles
and early church understood and obeyed their Lord's command.
Preaching was their preeminent ministry, and the gospel was their
preeminent theme. They literally devoted themselves "to prayer and
to the ministry of the word" (Acts 6:4). They would not divert from
this sacred task even when faced with other valid needs (6:1–4);
even when it was contrary to the laws of men (4:18–20); even when
it evoked the whip (5:40), the rod (16:22–23), stocks (16:24), chains
(12:6–7; 16:26; 21:33; 22:29; 26:29; 28:20), stones (7:58–60; 14:19),
and swords (12:2).

The primacy of gospel preaching is further revealed in the epis-
tles of the church's most prominent missionary, the apostle Paul.
The gospel was the message that he delivered as of first importance
(1 Cor. 15:3). Regardless of what cultures desired or men thought
they needed, Paul did not yield to their petitions but gave them the
only remedy prescribed by God. He wrote to the church in Corinth,
"Jews request a sign, and Greeks seek after wisdom; but we preach
Christ crucified…the power of God and the wisdom of God" (1 Cor.
1:22–24). Samuel Davies wrote,

"We preach Christ crucified!" The sufferings of Christ, which had a dreadful consummation in His crucifixion; their necessity, design, and consequences, and the way of salvation thereby opened for a guilty world these are the principal materials of our preaching! To instruct mankind in these, is the great object of our ministry, and the unwearied labor of our lives. We might easily choose subjects more pleasing and popular; more fit to display our learning and abilities, and set off the strong reasoner, or the fine orator; but our commission, as ministers of a crucified Jesus, binds us to the subject; and the necessity of the world peculiarly requires it![1]

Such was the prominence of the gospel in Paul's catalog of preaching themes that he declared to the church in Corinth, "I determined not to know anything among you except Jesus Christ and Him crucified" (1 Cor. 2:2). This does not mean that Paul did not expound on other matters of the Christian life, but he saw the gospel message as the very foundation on which the church was grounded and erected. If the church's understanding of the gospel was faulty to any degree, it would bring ruin to the entire edifice (1 Cor. 3:9–11). Thus, the gospel was the treasure of Paul's heart, the focal point of all his study, and the great theme of his preaching. Davies continued,

[The preaching of the gospel] was not the apostle's occasional practice, or a hasty wavering purpose; but he was determined upon it. "I determined," says he, "not to know any thing among you save Jesus Christ and him crucified!" [1 Cor. 2:2]. This theme, as it were, engrossed all his thoughts; he dwelt so much upon it, as if he had known nothing else and as if nothing else had been worth knowing! Indeed, he openly avows such a neglect and contempt of all other knowledge, in comparison to this: "I count all things but loss, for the excellency of the knowledge of Christ Jesus, my Lord!" [Phil. 3:8]. The crucifixion of Christ, which was the most ignominious circumstance in the whole course of His abasement, was an

---

1. Davies, *Sermons of Rev. Samuel Davies*, 1:621.

object in which Paul gloried; and he is struck with horror at the thought of glorying in any thing else! "God forbid," says he, "that I should glory, save in the cross of our Lord Jesus Christ!" [Gal. 6:14]. In short, he looked upon the cross as the perfection of his character as a Christian and an apostle, to be a constant student, and a zealous, indefatigable preacher of the cross of Christ![2]

D. Martyn Lloyd-Jones also taught on how vital it is to preach about Christ's work on the cross:

The preaching of the cross, the preaching of the death of the Lord Jesus Christ on that cross is the very heart and center of the Christian gospel and the Christian message. Now, I think you must all agree that that is an inevitable deduction, both from what the Apostle Paul says in Galatians 6:14 and from what he picks out as that in which he glories. The central thing, the thing that matters above everything else, and what he picks out is the cross, the death on the cross of our Lord Jesus Christ…. If you only preach the teaching of the Lord Jesus Christ, not only do you not solve the problem of mankind, in a sense you even aggravate it. You are preaching nothing but utter condemnation, because nobody can ever carry it out. So they (i.e. the apostles) did not preach His teaching. Paul does not say "God forbid that I should glory save in the ethical teaching of Jesus." He does not say that. It was not the teaching of Christ, nor the example of Christ either. That is often preached, is it not? "What is the message of Christianity? The imitation of Christ. Read the Gospels," they say, "and see how He lived. That is the way we all ought to live, so let us decide to do so. Let us decide to imitate Christ and to live as He lived." I say once more that that is not the center and the heart of the Christian message. That comes to it but not at the beginning. It is not the first thing, it is not the thing the apostles preached initially, neither was it our Lord's

2. Davies, *Sermons of Rev. Samuel Davies*, 1:621–22.

example. What they preached was His death upon the cross, and the meaning of that event.[3]

Oh fellow believers, the gospel is the great treasure of the Christian faith with which we have been entrusted (2 Cor. 4:7; 2 Tim. 1:14). We must devote ourselves to searching out its never-ending beauty and power, and we must preach it as those who are under the greatest and gravest stewardship. As Paul declared to Timothy shortly before his martyrdom, "I charge you therefore before God and the Lord Jesus Christ, who will judge the living and the dead at His appearing and His kingdom: Preach the word!" (2 Tim. 4:1–2).

The world's greatest need is the preaching of the gospel of Jesus Christ, "for it is the power of God to salvation for everyone who believes, for the Jew first and also for the Greek" (Rom. 1:16). The church's greatest need is the ongoing and ever deepening explanation and application of the gospel of Jesus Christ, for it is "the mystery of godliness"—the great revelation that results in true piety (1 Tim. 3:16). The apostle Paul had founded the church in Corinth. Nevertheless, in his first recorded letter to them, he wrote, "I declare to you the gospel which I preached to you, which also you received and in which you stand" (1 Cor. 15:1). Paul's constant desire was to teach the unfathomable riches of the gospel to the church, that it might stand with greater confidence in Christ and grow in conformity to His image. There is no theme of salvation or the Christian life that can be properly understood and expounded apart from the gospel. Thus, we must devote ourselves to its endless exploration and to the most faithful proclamation of its truths. As Richard Sibbes wrote,

> The object of preaching is especially Jesus Christ. This is the rock upon which the church is built. Christ should be the subject matter of our teaching, in His nature, offices, and benefits; in the duties which we owe to Him, and the instrument whereby we receive all from Him, which is faith.

---

3. David Martyn Lloyd-Jones, *The Cross: God's Way of Salvation* (Wheaton, Ill.: Crossway, 1986), 18–19, 20–21.

If we preach the law, and discover men's corruption, it is but to make way for the gospel's freer passage into their souls. And if we press holy duties, it is to make you walk worthy of the Lord Jesus. All teaching is reductive to the gospel of Christ, either to make way, as John Baptist did, to level all proud thoughts, and make us stoop to Him, or to make us walk worthy of the grace we receive from Him.

The bread of life must be broken; the sacrifice must be anatomized and laid open; the riches of Christ, even His "unsearchable riches," must be unfolded. "The Son of God," must be preached to all; and therefore God, who hath appointed us to be saved by Christ, hath also ordained preaching, to lay open the Lord Jesus, with the heavenly treasures of His grace and glory.[4]

4. Richard Sibbes, *The Works of Richard Sibbes, D.D.* (Edinburgh: Banner of Truth, 2017), 4:115–16.

11

THE PREEMINENT SUBJECT OF GLORYING

The gospel and the cross are the Christian's preeminent basis for glorying. Yet the word *preeminent* is too weak a word. The cross is so much more! It is the exclusive ground of the Christian's glory. This is well substantiated in Galatians 6:14, where the apostle Paul wrote, "But God forbid that I should boast except in the cross of our Lord Jesus Christ, by whom the world has been crucified to me, and I to the world."

In this text, the word *boast* is taken from the Greek verb *kaucháomai*, which means "to glory, exult, vaunt, or acclaim." Johannes Louw and Eugene Nida explain that it means "to express an unusually high degree of confidence in someone or something as being exceptionally noteworthy."[1] Thus, to glory in the cross of our Lord Jesus Christ is to make His vicarious and propitiatory death our confidence and boast—our one and only hope for salvation and the grand theme of our proclamation. It is to trust in Christ crucified as our "wisdom from God—and righteousness and sanctification and redemption" (1 Cor. 1:30) and to proclaim Him as the "reason for the hope that is in [us]" (1 Peter 3:15). As J. C. Ryle wrote,

> We can never attach too much importance to the atoning death of Christ. It is the leading fact in the word of God, on which the eyes of our soul ought to be ever fixed. Without the shedding of His blood, there is no remission of sin. It is

---

1. Johannes P. Louw and Eugene A. Nida, *Greek-English Lexicon of the New Testament: Based on Semantic Domains* (New York: United Bible Societies, 1989), 1:431.

the cardinal truth on which the whole system of Christianity hinges. Without it the gospel is an arch without a keystone, a fair building without a foundation, a solar system without a sun. Let us make much of our Lord's incarnation and example, His miracles and His parables, His works and His words, but above all let us make much of His death. Let us delight in the hope of His second personal coming and millennial reign, but let us not think more even of these blessed truths, than of the atonement on the cross. This, after all, is the master-truth of Scripture, that "Christ died for our sins." To this let us daily return. On this let us daily feed our souls. Some, like the Greeks of old, may sneer at the doctrine, and call it "foolishness." But let us never be ashamed to say with Paul, "God forbid that I should glory save in the cross of our Lord Jesus Christ."[2]

In Galatians 6:14, the apostle Paul used the strongest language possible to express his repugnance or abhorrence of placing anything above or on equal footing with the cross: "May it never be" (Greek: *emoì dè mē génoito*). He used a similar phrase in Romans 6:1–2 to express His detestation of the suggestion that a believer should give himself over to sin so that grace might be more manifest: "Shall we continue in sin that grace may abound? Certainly not!" In an attempt to communicate the force of the phrase, the KJV translates both texts "God forbid!" as though Paul were calling God to witness or making an oath to disavow any competition to the cross. The preposition *except* (Greek: *ei mē*) also serves to further emphasize the unchallenged preeminence of the cross in the Christian life. The cross is not one truth or theme among many; it holds the preeminence above them all. As Lloyd-Jones put it,

> The Christian not only glories in the cross, he glories in the cross alone. He glories in nothing else. Hear Isaac Watts putting it:

---

2. J. C. Ryle, *Expository Thoughts on Matthew* (Carlisle, Pa.: Banner of Truth, 2015), 347.

> Forbid it, Lord, that I should boast
> Save in the death of Christ my God.

There is an exclusiveness about the cross, which means that to the Christian this is the chiefest thing in history, the most important event that has ever taken place. It means that to him there is nothing which comes anywhere near it in significance. It means that he rests everything upon this, that this means all to him, that he is what he is because of this. He glorifies in it.[3]

Matthew Henry also speaks to the preeminence of the cross:

> This [cross] was what the Jews stumbled at and the Greeks accounted foolishness; and the judaizing teachers themselves, though they had embraced Christianity, yet were so far ashamed of it that in compliance with the Jews, and to avoid persecution from them, they were for mixing the observance of the law of Moses with faith in Christ, as necessary to salvation. But Paul had a very different opinion of it; he was so far from being offended at the cross of Christ, or ashamed of it, or afraid to own it, that he gloried in it; yea, he desired to glory in nothing else, and rejected the thought of setting up anything in competition with it, as the object of his esteem, with the utmost abhorrence; "God forbid," &c. This was the ground of all his hope as a Christian: this was the doctrine which, as an apostle, he was resolved to preach.[4]

Charles Spurgeon asked,

> "Why did Paul glory in the cross?" He did not do so because he was in want of a theme; for, as I have shown you, he had a wide field for boasting if he had chosen to occupy it. He gloried in the cross from solemn and deliberate choice. He had counted the cost, he had surveyed the whole range of subjects with eagle eye, and he knew what he did, and why he did

---

3. Lloyd-Jones, *Cross*, 54–55.
4. Henry, *Matthew Henry's Commentary*, 6:682–83.

it. He was master of the art of thinking. As a metaphysician, none could excel him; as a logical thinker, none could have gone beyond him. He stands almost alone in the early Christian church, as a master mind. Others may have been more poetic, or more simple, but none were more thoughtful or argumentative than he. With decision and firmness Paul sets aside everything else, and definitely declares, throughout his whole life, "I glory in the cross." He does this exclusively, saying, "God forbid that I should glory, save in the cross." There are many other precious things, but he puts them all upon the shelf in comparison with the cross. He will not even make his chief point any of the great scriptural doctrines, nor even an instructive and godly ordinance. No, the cross is to the front. This constellation is chief in Paul's sky. The choice of the cross he makes devoutly, for although the expression used in our English version may not stand, yet I do not doubt that Paul would have used it, and would have called upon God to witness that he abjured all other ground of glorying save the atoning sacrifice.

> "Forbid it, Lord, that I should boast, save in the death
> of Christ, my God; All the vain things that charm me
> most, I sacrifice them to his blood."

He would have called God to witness that he knew no ambition save that of bringing glory to the cross of Christ. As I think of this I am ready to say, "Amen" to Paul.[5]

It is important to note that when Paul declared that he boasted in nothing but the cross of Christ, he was not devaluing the rest of the Scriptures; rather, he was confirming the great purpose of Scripture. In John 5:39, Jesus declared to the Jews, "You search the Scriptures, for in them you think you have eternal life; and these are they which testify of Me." The whole of Scripture points to the cross and the Savior who died there as the fountainhead of our salvation. Without the cross, the entirety of the Scriptures would simply condemn us. Who

---

5. Spurgeon, *Metropolitan Tabernacle Pulpit*, 31:497.

has obeyed the law of God? Who has followed its precepts or adhered to its wisdom? Who has imitated the life of Christ so as to gain salvation through such imitation? The Scriptures declare, "No one!" The psalmist wrote, "If You, LORD, should mark iniquities, O Lord, who could stand?" (Ps. 130:3) and "Do not enter into judgment with Your servant, for in Your sight no one living is righteous" (Ps. 143:2). Wise Solomon lamented, "There is not a just man on earth who does good and does not sin" (Eccl. 7:20). The apostle Paul finalized our condemnation with the words, "For all have sinned and fall short of the glory of God" (Rom. 3:23). Therefore, it is not our obedience to the law, our imitation of Christ, the abstinence we have practiced, or the devotion we have shown to God that prevails. Our salvation is found in what God has accomplished on our behalf through the cross of His dear Son. It is for this reason, Lloyd-Jones wrote,

> The Apostle does not say: "God forbid that I should glory, save in the Sermon on the Mount, or in the teaching of the Lord Jesus Christ." The teaching of Christ condemned everybody, the Pharisees included, and showed everybody to be a complete and entire hopeless failure. So you do not glory in that. No, Paul glories in the cross, because it is through and from the cross that everything becomes possible, and all the blessings of the Christian life are laid open before us. The cross is the door that leads to all blessings. Without it there is nothing. Without the cross and all it means, we have no blessings from God at all. But the cross opens the possibility to all of the endless blessings of the glorious God.[6]

Dear reader, you who profess faith in Christ, do you comprehend Paul's dependence on the cross? Do you identify with his determination to confine all boasting to the singular event of the cross? Is it in the cross that you find your only source of righteousness, sanctification, and redemption (1 Cor. 1:30)? We must always remember that the mark of a true Christian is that he "[rejoices] in Christ Jesus, and

---

6. Lloyd-Jones, *Cross*, 177–78.

[has] no confidence in the flesh" (Phil. 3:3). Is this you? Lloyd-Jones continued,

> The Christian is a man who glories in the cross. If the cross is not central to you, you are not a Christian. You may say that you admire Jesus and His teaching, that does not make you a Christian. You can do that and be a Mohammedan. You can do that and still remain just a moralist. No, the cross is vital, the cross is central, everything comes out of it.[7]

> My dear friends, there never can be a more important question than this: What does this cross do to you? Where do you find yourself as you think of it and face it? It is one of these two, it is either an offense or else you glory in it. Are we all clear about our position? Do we know exactly where we stand? There are some perhaps saying, "Well quite certainly it is not an offense to me, but I am afraid I cannot say I glory in it." Well, my friend, you are in an impossible position. These are the only two positions—offense or glory.[8]

By the inspired writ of Scripture and the common confession of all genuine Christians, we are to glory in the cross of Christ alone. It is to be the alpha, omega, and middle letter of our theology, our faith, and our proclamation. This should never be doubted or disputed. But how can we assure ourselves that we are truly glorying in Christ and His cross alone? How do we avoid self-deception in the matter? In answer to this question, Charles Spurgeon wrote,

> If we do glory in the cross of Christ, how shall we prove it?
> *We must prove it by trusting in the cross.* The atonement must have our only confidence, or else it were vain to say that we glory in it. We must prove it, next, very holding fast the doctrine when others impugn it. We must be confident about this vicarious sacrifice of Christ, let others say what they may.

---

7. Lloyd-Jones, *Cross*, 199.
8. Lloyd-Jones, *Cross*, 41.

We must prove it by our zeal in propagating it according to the best of our ability. We must endeavor as much as lieth in us to tell the good news to others, that whosoever believeth hath everlasting life. But there are some here who are called to the ministry, and, therefore, to them let me say that we must prove that we glory in it almost by being prepared to suffer for it. Any man who is called to the ministry may, if he will take an example from yonder dome of St. Paul's Cathedral. There you see the cross above the globe. You must put from henceforth the cross above the world in all your calculations. To preach Jesus and to win souls, and not to gain money or human applause, must be the way in which you prove that you glory in the cross.

But the principal way is by constantly preaching about it. What shall I say to young men who are about to enter the ministry that shall be more useful to them than this? Keep to the cross; keep to the cross! Always preach up Jesus Christ! Always preach up Jesus Christ! I think no sermon should be without the doctrine of salvation by faith in it. I would not close a single discourse without at least something about believing in Jesus and living. Oh! that our tongues would speak of nothing but Jesus! Oh! that we were something like Rutherford, who is said to have had a squeaking voice on every other subject, but when he begun to speak of Christ the little man would grow tall and his voice become full, so that the duke who was one of his hearers called out, "Now man, you're on the right string!" Oh! surely, this is a theme that might inspire the very dumb, and make the dead to rise, to tell of Jesus Christ's most wondrous love.[9]

I will conclude this chapter with a strong and sincere admonition not only to keep the cross front and center in our theology but to devote ourselves to a lifetime of studying, contemplating, and preaching the cross. It is the preeminent revelation of God, the preeminent message of salvation and sanctification, the preeminent subject of

---

9. Spurgeon, *Metropolitan Tabernacle Pulpit*, 61:140–41.

study, and the preeminent theme of every kind of preaching. There are many important and wonderful themes to which readers may devote their time, intellect, and strength, but above them all is the theme of Calvary! Lloyd-Jones heartily agreed:

> Let us look again at the cross. Let us survey it once more. When a man like the apostle Paul glories in the cross you can be quite sure, my friend, that it is the biggest and the deepest and the profoundest thing in the whole universe. A casual glance at the cross is not enough. The saints of the centuries have been surveying it, they have been looking at it, gazing upon it, and meditating upon it. And the more they look at it the more they see in it. The writers of the hymns have done the same thing. The cross of Christ has produced some of the most magnificent poetry in the English language. But the writers have looked at it, they have surveyed it, they have not just said, "Oh yes, I know Jesus died, He was a pacifist, and He died"—and then gone on indifferently. Neither have they said something like some of us perhaps—Christian people, evangelical people—"Oh yes, I believe in the cross, I believe Christ died for me," and then thought no more about it. Oh, my dear friend, if that is how it affects you, you have not seen the cross. You must stop and look, survey, put everything else on one side and gaze at it, and don't stop looking at it until you have seen some of these profundities—or what Thomas Carlisle described in another connection, "infinities and immensities"—in this glorious cross.[10]

William Romaine also gloried in our Redeemer's sacrifice for us:

> Christ's dying love we should keep ever in mind; we should have it always warm upon our hearts, and always upon our tongues. His passion on the tree is our never ceasing theme: "God forbid that we should glory, except in the cross of our Lord Jesus Christ" [Gal. 6:14]. In this we glory, and in this alone, with our voices, and with every musical instrument,

---

10. Lloyd-Jones, *Cross*, 64–65.

but chiefly with the melody of our hearts, we endeavour to praise Him, who was slain, and hath redeemed us unto God by His blood.[11]

11. Adapted from William Romaine, *Essay on Psalmody* (London, 1775).

12

A WARNING AGAINST THE NEGLECT OF THE GOSPEL

Given the extraordinary nature of the gospel of Jesus Christ and the solemn stewardship that has been given to us, it is only fitting that I provide a warning as we draw near the end of this book. We must beware of any degree of apathy or neglect with regard to the gospel, our study of its wonders, and our proclamation of its truths. Hebrews 2:1–3 warns, "We must give the more earnest heed to the things we have heard [i.e., the gospel], lest we drift away. For if the word spoken through angels [i.e., the law] proved steadfast, and every transgression and disobedience received a just reward, how shall we escape if we neglect so great a salvation…?"

Later in the book of Hebrews, the Holy Spirit is even more forceful: "Anyone who has rejected Moses' law dies without mercy on the testimony of two or three witnesses. Of how much worse punishment, do you suppose, will he be thought worthy who has trampled the Son of God underfoot, counted the blood of the covenant by which he was sanctified a common thing, and insulted the Spirit of grace?" (Heb. 10:28–29).

In the immediate context the writer of Hebrews is warning against apostasy—a settled or chronic rejection of the gospel. Nevertheless, the warning may be applied in limited degrees to any form of apathy or neglect. Correct theology is essential, but it is not enough. We must be on constant guard against losing our first love for Christ and our initial appreciation for His gospel. Christ's warning to the church in Ephesus is a painful but helpful reminder: "Nevertheless I have this against you, that you have left your first love. Remember therefore from where you have fallen; repent and do the first works, or else I will come to you quickly and remove your lampstand from its place—unless you repent" (Rev. 2:4–5).

The genuine Christian—the truly regenerate heart—will have strong affections for Christ and His gospel. However, even the most sanctified Christian is still subject to the inclinations of the fallen flesh and the temptations of the devil, who works relentlessly to divert the believer's attention and affections to lesser things. Paul wrote to the believers in Corinth who were enticed by the preaching of another Jesus, "But I fear, lest somehow, as the serpent deceived Eve by his craftiness, so your minds may be corrupted from the simplicity that is in Christ" (2 Cor. 11:3). He wrote to the believers in Galatia who were beginning to stray from the gospel, "O foolish Galatians! Who has bewitched you that you should not obey the truth, before whose eyes Jesus Christ was clearly portrayed among you as crucified?" (Gal. 3:1). He warned the believers in Colossae who were badgered by false teachers, "Beware lest anyone cheat you through philosophy and empty deceit, according to the tradition of men, according to the basic principles of the world, and not according to Christ" (Col. 2:8).

Dear reader, you must always be on guard against the heresies that will seek to divert your attention from the gospel. However, you must exercise even greater caution against those things that are good and biblical but are no replacement for the gospel. They may point to the gospel or flow from it, but they are not the gospel and do not equal it in preeminence. Paul wrote, "The law is holy, and the commandment holy and just and good" (Rom. 7:12). Nevertheless, it is the shadow and not the substance. It does not save; its function is to point to the Savior. Marriage and family are ordained of God and are great expressions of His grace. Nevertheless, they are not the centerpiece of Christianity. Ethics, virtue, and morality are matters of great importance in the Christian life and can give great evidence to the power of the gospel, but if they are given precedence or even equal rank with the gospel, they become dangerous distractions. Finally, the temporal gifts without number that God gives to His people are to be received with gratitude. Yet the greatest of them is but dust compared to His only begotten Son. The gift of a thousand worlds would be rubbish compared to Christ. For this reason, John Flavel warned, "O beware, lest the dust of the earth, getting into thine eyes, so blind thee, that thou never see the beauty or necessity of Christ."[1]

All that we have read thus far should lead us to a very practical question: How can we avoid neglect and grow in our appreciation for and devotion to the gospel? The answer comes in several parts.

Learn the Greatness of the Theme

When we make reference to the gospel, we are not calling attention to *a theme* in Scripture but to *the theme* of Scripture and, dare we say, the most prominent thought in the mind of God. Many of the old saints have said that the very dust of the Bible is gold. How much more precious, then, is its greatest treasure? We must not be mistaken: nothing equals the gospel in value, nothing matches its wisdom, and nothing compares with its beauty. Borrowing from the wise man's description of wisdom we may say, "Her proceeds are better than the profits of silver, and her gain than fine gold. She is more precious than rubies, and all the things you may desire cannot compare with her" (Prov. 3:14–15). William Bates wrote,

> The doctrine of the gospel exceeds all practical sciences in the excellency of its end, and the efficacy of the means to obtain it. The end of it is, the supreme happiness of man; the restoring of him to the innocence and excellency of his first state. And the means are appointed by infinite wisdom, so that the most insuperable obstacles are removed, and these are the justice of God that condemns the guilty, and that strong and obstinate aversion which is in corrupted man.... Here is a Mediator revealed, who is "able to save to the uttermost"; who hath quenched the wrath of God by the blood of His divine sacrifice: who hath expiated sin by the value of His death, and purifies the soul by the virtue of His life, that it may consent to its own salvation. No less than a divine power could perform

---

1. Flavel, *Works of John Flavel*, 1:26.

this work. From hence the superlative excellency of evangelical knowledge doth arise; all other knowledge is unprofitable
without it, and it alone can make us perfectly blessed; "This is
life eternal, to know thee, and Jesus Christ, whom thou hast
sent" [John 17:3].[2]

Be Provoked by Greater Hearts

Christianity is not a "lone wolf" religion. The Scriptures are adamant
that we need one another to remain steadfast in the faith and grow
in grace. Proverbs 27:17 declares, "As iron sharpens iron, so a man
sharpens the countenance of his friend." The writer of Hebrews is
even more explicit: "Let us hold fast the confession of our hope without wavering, for He who promised is faithful. And let us consider
one another in order to stir up love and good works, not forsaking
the assembling of ourselves together, as is the manner of some, but
exhorting one another, and so much the more as you see the Day
approaching" (Heb. 10:23–25).

Even the great apostle Paul was aware of his own need. In Romans
1:11–12, he wrote to the church in Rome, "For I long to see you…
that I may be encouraged together with you by the mutual faith both
of you and me." The Scriptures prove that we need one another to
progress in all matters of the faith. However, what can we do when
we find ourselves in the midst of a Christianity that is out of focus,
that has set its looking glass to matters of lesser importance, and that
does not see the gospel clearly? Three things are recommended.

First, to provoke our hearts to greater devotion to Christ, we
should seek encouragement in the Scriptures, where we will find
hearts and minds set on fire for Christ and His gospel. According to
1 Peter 1:12, the same seraphim who covered their faces before the
throne of God (Isa. 6:1–3) are now longing to look at all the magnificent wonders that are found without measure in the gospel. The
phrase "to long" is translated from the Greek verb *epithuméō*, which
means "to set one's heart on something," "to desire earnestly," even

---

2. Bates, *Harmony of the Divine Attributes*, 105.

"to lust after or covet." The phrase "to look" is translated from the Greek verb *parakútō*, which literally means "to lean in" or "stoop down." The gospel must be exceedingly great if angels desire to turn from other matters to peer into it and labor with their great minds to comprehend it! Should not their response provoke us to a greater passion to do the same? If the most noble creatures in all of creation find their greatest delight in peering into the gospel, should we not leave aside ignoble things and join them in their nobility? William Bates wrote,

> We content ourselves with slight and transient glances, but do not seriously and fixedly consider this blessed design of God, upon which the beginning of our happiness in this, and the perfection of it in the next life, is built. Let us provoke ourselves by the example of the angels who are not concerned in this redemption as man is; for they continued in their fidelity to their Creator, and were always happy in His favor; and where there is no alienation between parties, reconcilement is unnecessary; yet they are students with us in the same book, and unite all their powers in the contemplation of this mystery: they are represented stooping to pry into these secrets, to signify their delight in what they know, and their desire to advance in the knowledge of them [1 Peter 1:12]. With what intentness then should we study the gospel, who are the subject and end of it![3]

In the Scriptures, we are spurred on not only by angels but also by example after example of saints who possessed an extraordinary passion to catch even the slightest glimpse of God's redemptive plan. By faith, Abraham rejoiced to see Christ's day through the promises that were given to him (John 8:56). Moses considered the reproach of Christ "greater riches than the treasures in Egypt" (Heb. 11:26). The prophets "inquired and searched carefully, who prophesied of the grace that would come to you, searching what, or what manner of time, the Spirit of Christ who was in them was indicating when

---

3. Bates, *Harmony of the Divine Attributes*, 110.

He testified beforehand the sufferings of Christ and the glories that would follow" (1 Peter 1:10–11). The pagan magi traveled far from their homeland just to see the babe and lay treasures at His feet (Matt. 2:1–2, 9–11). The widow Anna "did not depart from the temple, but served God with fastings and prayers night and day" as she waited for the salvation that was to come through the Messiah. When she finally beheld Him, she "gave thanks to the Lord, and spoke of Him to all those who looked for redemption in Jerusalem" (Luke 2:37–38). Righteous Simeon took Jesus in his arms and declared that the whole ambition of his life had been fulfilled and he was ready to die: "Lord, now You are letting Your servant depart in peace, according to Your word; for my eyes have seen Your salvation" (Luke 2:29–30). Finally, the apostle Paul, voicing what was surely the desire of the entire apostolic band, declared, "But what things were gain to me, these I have counted loss for Christ. Yet indeed I also count all things loss for the excellence of the knowledge of Christ Jesus my Lord, for whom I have suffered the loss of all things, and count them as rubbish, that I may gain Christ" (Phil. 3:7–8).

We should also seek encouragement from churches and ministers who love Christ and His gospel. We must never succumb to Elijah's doubt, thinking that we are the only ones left who are faithful in Israel. We must remember that God will always reserve for Himself a remnant much larger than we could ever imagine (1 Kings 19:10–14). We should make every attempt to seek out a biblical church and become committed members of its fellowship. Such a church will be known by its high view of God, its submission to the Scriptures, and its love for Christ and His gospel. Such a church will make much of Christ and count all things as rubbish (especially temporal prosperity) in comparison to Him.

Finally, we should look to the history of the church. Many godly men and women are scattered throughout church history, and their writings are a literal ocean of biblical knowledge and wonderful insights into the excellencies of Christ. Especially noteworthy are the writings of the Reformers, the Puritans, the Particular Baptists, and the early evangelicals. Like all writings outside of the Scriptures, these works are not infallible and so must be tested, but their authors exhibit a knowledge of the Scriptures and an ability to expound them that is rarely found among us today. One of the finest examples of such gospel-saturated saints is Isaac Ambrose. His following two admonitions demonstrate the power of ancient writers to provoke us to a higher devotion to Christ:

> O that I should need thus to persuade your hearts to look unto Jesus! What, is not your Jesus worthy of this? Why, then, are your thoughts no more upon Him? Why are not your hearts continually with Him? Why are not your strongest desires, and daily delights in, and after the Lord Jesus? What is the matter? Will not God give you leave to approach this light? Will He not suffer your souls to taste and see? Why then doth He cry, and double His cry, "Behold me, behold me" [Isa. 65:1]? Ah, vile hearts! How delightfully and unweariedly can we think of vanity? How freely and how frequently can we think of our pleasures, friends, labors, lusts? Yea, of our miseries, wrongs, sufferings, fear? And what, is not Christ in all our thoughts? It was said of the Jews, that they used to cast to the ground the book of Esther before they read it, because the name of God was not in it; and Augustine cast by Cicero's writings, because they contained not the name of Jesus. Christians! Thus should you humble and cast down your sensual hearts, that have in them no more of Christ: O chide them for their willful or weak strangeness to Jesus Christ! O turn your thoughts from off all earthly vanities, and bend your souls to study Christ; habituate yourselves to such contemplations; and let not these thoughts be seldom or cursory, but settle upon them, dwell there, bathe your souls in those delights, drench your affections in those rivers of pleasures, or rather in the sea of consolation. O tie your souls in heavenly galleries, have your eyes continually set on Christ![4]

---

4. Ambrose, *Looking unto Jesus*, 32–33.

The most excellent subject to discourse or write of, is Jesus Christ. Augustine, having read Cicero's works, commended them for their eloquence; but he passed this sentence upon them, "They are not sweet, because the name of Jesus is not in them." And Bernard's saying is near the same, "If thou writest, it doth not relish well with me, unless Jesus sound there." Indeed all we say is but unsavory, if it be not seasoned with this salt, "I determined not to know anything among you, (saith Paul,) save Jesus Christ, and him crucified."[5]

Accept Rebuke from Those Who Show Greater Devotion to Lesser Things

The book of Proverbs teaches us that we may learn from the fool as well as the wise. Throughout history men have shown more dedication to folly than we do to the greatest matter of all—the gospel of Jesus Christ. In the following we will survey such examples, accept their rebuke, and allow them to spur us on to greater devotion to the only One who is deserving of all devotion from men and angels.

The book of Malachi is the last word from God for more than four hundred years, until the coming of the Messiah. The context of this prophecy is Israel's blindness to God's goodness toward them, resulting in ingratitude, apathy, and disobedience. In Malachi 1:6-8, God points to the common customs of the world to rebuke His people:

> "A son honors his father, and a servant his master. If then I am the Father, where is My honor? And if I am a Master, where is My reverence? says the LORD of hosts to you priests who despise My name. Yet you say, 'In what way have we despised Your name?' You offer defiled food on My altar, but say, 'In what way have we defiled You?' By saying, 'The table of the LORD is contemptible.' And when you offer the blind as a sacrifice, is it not evil? And when you offer the lame and sick, is it not evil? Offer it then to your governor! Would he be pleased

---

5. Ambrose, *Looking unto Jesus*, 17.

with you? Would he accept you favorably?" says the LORD of hosts.

The above questions should cut each one of us to the quick. A son honors his father because he is his progenitor and provider. A servant honors his master because he is indebted to him. A citizen offers his best to the governor because of his station above him as ruler and protector. Yet who are these compared to God, and what is any obligation to them in comparison to our obligation to God, who "did not spare His own Son, but delivered Him up for us all," and "freely give[s] us all things" (Rom. 8:32)? "Scarcely for a righteous man will one die; yet perhaps for a good man someone would even dare to die. But God demonstrates His own love toward us, in that while we were still sinners, Christ died for us" (Rom. 5:7–8). How great is our indebtedness to God for what He has done for us through His Son. Does it not deserve far more than a nod of the head, a few meager moments of contemplation, or miserly sacrifices of little cost to us? Does it not demand that Christ and His gospel be the very center of our thoughts and that thanks be given to Him with every beat of the heart? What is a sunset, an ocean, the stars, the riches of this world compared to Christ? What are mansions of glory and streets of gold compared to Christ? If men can spend themselves for lesser things, should we not spend ourselves for the greater? Charles Spurgeon wrote,

> What myriads of eyes are casting their glances at the sun! What multitudes of men lift up their eyes, and behold the starry orbs of heaven! They are continually watched by thousands—but there is one great transaction in the world's history, which everyday commands far more spectators than that sun which goeth forth like a bridegroom, strong to run his race. There is one great event, which every day attracts more admiration than do the sun, and moon, and stars, when they march in their courses. That event is, the death of our Lord Jesus Christ. To it, the eyes of all the saints who lived before the Christian era were always directed; and backwards, through the thousand years of history, the eyes of all

modern saints are looking. Upon Christ, the angels in heaven perpetually gaze. "Which things the angels desire to look into," said the apostle. Upon Christ, the myriad eyes of the redeemed are perpetually fixed; and thousands of pilgrims, through this world of tears, have no higher object for their faith, and no better desire for their vision, than to see Christ as He is in heaven, and in communion to behold His person. Beloved, we shall have many with us, whilst we turn our face to the Mount of Calvary. We shall not be solitary spectators of the fearful tragedy of our Saviour's death: we shall but dart our eyes to that place which is the focus of heaven's joy and delight, the cross of our Lord and Saviour Jesus Christ.[6]

In 1 Corinthians 9:25, Paul gave us a powerful example of those who give their all to obtain that which is perishable: "Everyone who competes for the prize is temperate in all things. Now they do it to obtain a perishable crown, but we for an imperishable crown." We admire the modern-day Olympians who devote their entire lives for a single chance to gain a medal that perishes and a fame that quickly fades. We esteem the writers, painters, and other artists who labor their entire lives in anonymity and poverty simply to express beauty. We hold in high regard the scientists, mathematicians, and philosophers who lock themselves away and push their minds to the limit to know what can be known. We applaud the explorers who make untold sacrifices and pass through grievous hardships simply to discover the unknown. Are they not all a rebuke to the Christian who has been given the opportunity to devote his or her entire life to seeking out the glories of God in the person and work of Christ, to be transformed by them, and to make them known? If others can show extraordinary discipline for the temporal and the finite, shall we not discipline ourselves for the eternal and infinite? As John Flavel wrote,

6. Charles Spurgeon, *The New Park Street Pulpit* (Pasadena, Tex.: Pilgrim Publications, 1981), 4:65.

There is no doctrine more excellent in itself, or more necessary to be preached and studied, than the doctrine of Jesus Christ, and Him crucified. All other knowledge, how much soever it be magnified in the world, is, and ought to be esteemed but dross, in comparison of the excellency of the knowledge of Jesus Christ [Phil. 3:8]. "In him are hid all the treasures of wisdom and knowledge" [Col. 2:3]. Eudoxus was so affected with the glory of the sun, that he thought he was born only to behold it; much more should a Christian judge himself born only to behold and delight in the glory of the Lord Jesus.[7]

Isaac Ambrose also noted,

It is not enough to study and know Him, but according to the measure of knowledge we have attained, we must ponder, and muse, and meditate, and consider of Him: now, consideration is an expatiating and enlarging of the mind and heart on this or that subject. Consideration is a fixing of our thoughts, a steadfast bending of our minds to some spiritual matter, till it work in the affections and conversation. We may know, and yet be inconsiderate of that we do know, but when the intention of our mind and heart is taken up about some known object, and other things are not for the present taken notice of, this is consideration. Oh that, if it were possible we could so consider Jesus in this first period of eternity, as that for a while at least we could forget all other things! Christian, I beseech you be dead to the world, be insensible of all other things, and look only to Jesus. It is said that men in a frenzy are insensible of what you do to them, because their minds are taken up about that which they apprehend so strongly; and if ever there was an object made known to take up the mind of a spiritual man, it is this, even this—Christ! It is reported of one Archimedes, who was a great mathematician, that when the city was taken wherein he was, and the warlike instruments of death clattering about his ears, and all was in

---

7. Flavel, *Works of John Flavel*, 1:34.

a tumult, yet he was so busy about drawing his lines, that he heard no noise, nor did he know that there was any danger. But if such objects as those could take up the intentions of his mind, so as not to regard other things, how much more should this consideration of Christ. If a carnal heart, a man that minds earthly things, be so taken up about them, because they are an object suitable to him; how much more should a gracious heart, that can see into the reality of these things of God and Christ from everlasting, be so taken up with them as to mind nothing else. Come then, Oh my soul, and set thy consideration on work.... There is not any piece of this transaction but it is of special use, and worth thy pains. How many break their brains, and waste their spirits in studying arts and sciences, things in comparison of no value; whereas Paul otherwise "determined not to know any thing among you but Jesus Christ" [1 Cor. 2:2]?... To know Jesus Christ in every piece and point, whether in birth, or life, or death, it is saving knowledge: Oh stand not upon cost, whether pains or study, tears or prayers, peace or wealth, goods or name, life or liberty, sell all for this pearl: Christ is of that worth and use, that thou canst never over-buy Him, though thou gavest thyself and all the world for Him; the study of Christ is the study of studies; the knowledge of Christ is the knowledge of everything that is necessary either for this world, or for the world to come. Oh study Christ.[8]

William Bates, in *The Harmony of the Divine Attributes*, likewise commented on this theme:

Seneca, a philosopher and a courtier, valued his being in the world only upon this account, that he might contemplate the starry heaven. He only saw the visible beauty of the firmament, but was ignorant of the glory within it, and of the way that leads to it; yet, to our shame, he speaks that the sight of it made him despise the earth, and without the contemplation

---

8. Ambrose, *Looking unto Jesus*, 65–66, 196.

of the celestial bodies, he esteemed his continuance in the world not the life of a man, but the toil of a beast.[9]

Deal Severely with the Slightest Apathy

Some matters in the Christian life must be dealt with urgently and severely. A heart that is apathetic and lethargic in seeking to know Christ is one of them. In Matthew 5:29–30, Jesus gave one of His strongest and most radical admonitions: "If your right eye causes you to sin, pluck it out and cast it from you.... And if your right hand causes you to sin, cut it off and cast it from you." Although He was speaking in hyperbole, the point should be well taken. Sinful actions and attitudes of the heart should be dealt with most severely, lest they bring severe discipline. In Revelation 2:5, Jesus warned the church in Ephesus that had left its first love, "Remember therefore from where you have fallen; repent and do the first works, or else I will come to you quickly and remove your lampstand from its place—unless you repent." We seem prone to make distinctions between greater and lesser sins. We rightly view murder and immorality to be heinous violations of the law of God, and thus we fear them and set up parameters to guard ourselves from falling. If perchance we or another fall into such a grievous sin, we are filled with shame and lamentation. However, we oftentimes wrongly view other sins that produce less public scandal as more bearable. Yet is not an apathy for Christ and His gospel the root of all other kinds of sin? Is it not the beginning of the slide? Is it not a Pandora's box that, when opened, brings many dangers?

When we find ourselves with a lukewarm heart toward Christ and His redemptive work on our behalf, we must deal with ourselves in the most severe manner. We must acknowledge that we are acting stupidly and that our neglect is nothing short of madness. Then, we must make an immediate counterattack through repentance, renewal of our commitment, saturating our lives in the Word of God and prayer, and seeking godly fellowship. As Edward Payson wrote,

9. Bates, *Harmony of the Divine Attributes*, 109.

There cannot, my friends, be a more striking and satisfactory proof of our stupid insensibility to religious truth, than the indifference with which we naturally view the gospel of Christ. Among all the wonderful things which God has presented to the contemplation of His creatures, none are so well suited to excite our deepest interest and attention, as those which this gospel reveals.[10]

William Bates also concurred with the gravity of seeking the gospel above all earthly pursuits:

With greater reason we may wonder, that men should, with the expense of their precious hours, purchase barren curiosities, which are unprofitable to their last end. How can a condemned criminal, who is in suspense between life and death, attend to study the secrets of nature and art, when all his thoughts are taken up how to prevent the execution of the sentence? And it is no less than a prodigy of madness, that men who have but a short and uncertain space allowed them to escape the wrath to come, should rack their brains in studying things impertinent to salvation, and neglect the knowledge of a Redeemer. Especially when there is so clear a revelation of Him: the righteousness of faith doth not command us to ascend to the heavens, or descend into the deep to make a discovery of it; but the word is nigh us, that discovers the certain way to a happy immortality [Rom. 10:6–7].[11]

---

10. Payson, *Complete Works of Edward Payson*, 3:148.
11. Bates, *Harmony of the Divine Attributes*, 109.

13

FINAL EXHORTATION

Oh dear brothers and sisters in Christ, what more can I say than what has been said to your heart and mind? Is not an accurate description of Christ's glory beyond the possibility of language—human or angelic? Does not even our meager knowledge of Christ exceed all expectations? Are not the greatest themes of every academic discipline nothing more than foothills to His mountain? Can anyone be set beside Him without shame? As Flavel teaches us, "All fair things, [are] black, deformed, and without beauty, when they are set beside the fairest Lord Jesus!"[1]

I plead with you as I plead with my own heart to seek the glory of God in the gospel of Christ. Make it your life discipline and your daily practice. Is there anyone or anything more worthy of your devotion, your time, your strength, your life? There is not! You know that there is not! If you are a believer, you know He has proved Himself to you over and over again. Every time you have foolishly chased after other loves, you have found yourself empty, soiled, worn, and longing. Every time you have returned to Him, you have found Him beyond expectations in mercy, compassion, and love.

Let us then make a strong determination, and renew it every day, to seek our Savior and discover the greatness of His person and deeds—the life He lived, the things He suffered, the victories He won, and the salvation He accomplished on our behalf. Let us go deeper, higher, and stay longer in our private meetings with Him. Shall we

---

1. Flavel, *Works of John Flavel*, 1:xix–xx.

neglect to take full advantage of an audience with a king—and such a King as this? The world seeks us and freely offers us its uncut and worthless stones. Will we allow these trinkets to turn us away from seeking the diamonds of heaven? We must pull away from the vanity fairs of this world and all their amusements and follow the narrow path to glory, for "the path of the just is like the shining sun, that shines ever brighter unto the perfect day" (Prov. 4:18). Although at times we must walk in darkness and have no light, let us trust in the name of the Lord and rely on our God (Isa. 50:10). Darkness will eventually give way to shadow, and shadow to light, and light to the full day. If we set ourselves to seek Him, our seeking will not be in vain. The prophet Hosea's exhortation, "Let us know, let us pursue the knowledge of the LORD," is followed by a promise: "His going forth is established as the morning; He will come to us like the rain, like the latter and former rain to the earth" (Hos. 6:3). The exhortation is literally, "Let us pursue in order to know." Let us track Him as a hunter tracks a stag. Let us pursue Him in a marvelous chase. Then, once He lets us catch Him, let us join with Jacob and Moses in the bold demand, "I will not let You go until You bless me with a greater display of Your glory!" (see Gen. 32:26; Ex. 33:18).

You may ask, "Dare we speak with such boldness concerning our Lord? Can we be certain that He will meet with us?" Hosea answers, "His going forth is established as the morning; He will come to us like the rain, like the latter and former rain to the earth." Do you believe the sun will rise tomorrow, bringing the dawn and a new day? Then reason demands that you believe with greater certainty that Christ not only will come to you but will come as a spring rain watering your soul. The Lord's willingness to be found by those who seek Him is the certainty of certainties. He told Jeremiah, "You will seek Me and find Me, when you search for Me with all your heart" (Jer. 29:13). David counseled Solomon, "If you seek Him, He will be found by you" (1 Chron. 28:9). These promises are not the exclusive right of prophets, kings, and martyrs; they belong even to the wayward among God's people. God promised Israel that He would be found by them even in exile: "But from there you will seek the LORD your God, and you will find Him if you seek Him with all your heart and with all your soul" (Deut. 4:29). God extends this promise even further through His prophet Isaiah: "I was sought by those who did not ask for Me; I was found by those who did not seek Me. I said, 'Here I am, here I am,' to a nation that was not called by My name" (Isa. 65:1). Having these promises, let us be urgent to "seek the LORD while He may be found, call upon Him while He is near" (Isa. 55:6). If we have tasted and seen that the Lord is good (Ps. 34:8), let us tarry longer at His table, that we may see and savor more and more of Him each day.

To conclude, I leave you with the words of men more knowledgeable than I, that they might renew your zeal to seek Christ in the gospel and strengthen your commitment with an unbreakable cord:

> Oh! how should all hearts be taken with this Christ? Christians! Turn your eyes upon the Lord. "Look, and look again unto Jesus." Why stand ye gazing on the toys of this world, when such a Christ is offered to you in the gospel? Can the world die for you? Can the world reconcile you to the Father? Can the world advance you to the kingdom of heaven? As Christ is all in all, so let Him be the full and complete subject of our desire, and hope, and faith, and love, and joy; let Him be in your thoughts the first in the morning, and the last at night. Shall I speak one word more to thee that believest? Oh! apply in particular all the transactions of Jesus Christ to thy very self; remember how He came out of His Father's bosom for thee, wept for thee, bled for thee, poured out His life for thee, is now risen for thee, gone to heaven for thee, sits at God's right hand, and rules all the world for thee, makes intercession for thee, and at the end of the world will come again for thee, and receive thee to Himself, to live with Him for ever and ever. Surely if thus thou believest and livest, thy life is comfortable, and thy death will be sweet. If there be any heaven upon earth, thou wilt find it in the practice and exercise of this gospel duty, in "Looking unto Jesus."[2]

---

2. Ambrose, *Looking unto Jesus*, 694.

Whenever we attain to any serious thoughts of that great business of our redemption by Christ incarnate and crucified, we should not suffer our hearts to be soon diverted from them, but should labour to dwell upon them and to search out more and more considerations of that sweet subject, every one of them being worthy to take up our affections and to engage us to the study of holiness.[3]

Dear Sir, Christ is the peerless pearl hid in the field [Matt. 13:46]. Will you be that wise merchant, that resolves to win and compass that treasure, whatever it shall cost you? Ah, Sir, Christ is a commodity that can never be bought too dear.[4]

---

3. Alexander Nisbet, *Geneva Series Commentaries: An Exposition of I & II Peter* (Carlisle, Pa.: Banner of Truth, 1982), 46.

4. John Flavel, *The Fountain of Life Opened Up*, ed. Anthony Uyl (Woodstock, Ontario: Devoted Publishing, 2018), 5.